Expect F*cking More

The 5 Keys to Business Success for African American Women

Dr. Bee Thomas

ISBN: 978-1-7352287-0-9

Dedication

This book is dedicated to my ancestors and to all African American women business owners.

Acknowledgements

A special thank you to my editor Dr. Charlie from Edit 911

Photographer, Debora Barreto

Cover Art Designer, E. R. Canedo

Inside Art Designer, Umit Arat and Merc Design

An incredibly special thank you to my love Matt Sibert. Without your support where would I be? Thank you for helping me birth our baby, this book! And last but not least, thank you to my mother and father who continue to support my growth.

Sending my love to all business owners who dare to dream big!

Contents

Introduction

African American Women Take Over. Hear ye! Hear ye! There is a shift in the atmosphere. The year is 2020. Are you the next African American female Bill Gates in the making? Better yet, are you the next *you* in the making? The time has come for you and *your business* to take center stage. This shift is the alarm to grow your business in ways you never imagined, to throw off restrictions. It's not good enough to have a "seat at the table" of business ownership and accept mediocre results. It's time for you to own the table, building, and block. Business is a game, and success is a reward. I am here to light a fire under you! I am here to get you into the game of business and develop the attitude of play to win—like the MVPs. You can achieve success in remarkable ways that supersede your wildest imagination. All you need are the tools and the know-how. In this book, I give you the keys you need to start and increase your business success. Yet, before I give you the keys, let's get acquainted with our topic, business.

Part I: Your Time to Shine

African American Women and Business

The Good

In the last 12 years, Black women business owners launched more firms than all other ethnicities. Between 2007 and 2018, African American women-owned businesses (AAWOB) grew by a stunning 164%, three times the rate of all women-owned firms, which grew an impressive 58% during that same timeframe.[1] From 2017 to 2018, African American Women (AAW) launched an astonishing 541 businesses per day, higher than all women business owners. Comparatively, Latina women started 401 businesses per day.[1] By 2018, there were 2.4 million reported AAWOB. As of 2018, African American women business owners (AAWBO) accounted for 20% of all women-owned businesses, and that number is growing. African American Women are the only ethnic group (of women business owners), with more business owners than their male peers.

The Bad

African American women-owned businesses are showing growth in various areas of development (including business quantity, steady employment, and profit). However, African American women realize marginalized profits and decreased business success compared to other minority and nonminority business owners.[2] Researchers do not agree on an explanation for this African American female entrepreneur phenomenon. Although African American women are slightly more likely to start a business compared to White women, the number of firms owned by African American women trail White women-owned businesses.[3] Increased African American female entrepreneurialism, and dwindling numbers of African American female-owned businesses, may indicate decreased survival rates. Research concerning the African American female entrepreneurial experience is limited.

The Ugly

The average revenue of an AAWBO is $24,700 per firm compared to $143,100 (the average revenue, per firm, for all women-owned businesses). Also, from 2007 to 2018, the average revenue dropped for women of color businesses from $84,100 to $66,400. However, during the same timeframe the average revenue rose for a non-minority business from $181,000 to $212,300.[1] The average revenue gap between AAWBO and all women owned businesses is the greatest.

"If revenues generated by minority women-owned firms matched those currently generated by all women-owned businesses, they would add four million new jobs and $1.2 trillion in revenues to the U.S. economy." [1]

The revenue gap is growing between African American women business owners-and all women-owned businesses. Statistics also suggest that African American women hire fewer employees, averaging .02 vs. the average of all women-owned firms of 7 employees. This statistic is a red flag and a predictor of business failure. Businesses without employees are three times more likely to close compared to firms with employees. Business growth and expansion are often contingent on human and financial capital.

"Growth in both employment and revenues begins to take off for women-owned businesses when they reach $250,000 in revenues. Supporting businesses on the cusp of crossing this threshold ($100,000 to $249,999), and those that have crossed it, could accelerate the growth of larger women-owned businesses.[1]"

An immense disparity continues between gender and African American entrepreneurial success compared to the success of White business owners.[4]

African American female entrepreneurs have influenced the American economy. Yet, despite their success, African American women business owners may suffer dual discrimination as Black Women[5].

Entrepreneurship: The American Dream

Entrepreneurialism is the concept of creating a product or service for public consumption. Entrepreneurialism in America started with small mom-and-pop stores set up by various ethnic groups who migrated to America. Business researchers view entrepreneurialism as a portal to achieving the American dream of independence and as a critical part of the American economy.[6] Puryear confirmed the economic importance of entrepreneurialism within the United States, indicating that entrepreneurialism provides "(1) a mainstay of economic growth and job creation, (2) approving ground for product and service innovations, and (3) a means of identifying and exploited previously underdeveloped markets" (p. 423).[7]

America, built on the entrepreneurial spirit since its birth, has thrived on the success of innovation through entrepreneurial thinkers. Thus, entrepreneurialism is a necessary resource—crucial for guiding America through global change.[6] Additionally, entrepreneurialism supports the American economy by supplying jobs and product innovations.[8] A lack of entrepreneurialism in America would threaten the economy and affect America's economic ability to compete as a global financial leader.[9] The underrepresentation of African American businesses within American society limits economic growth and job creation opportunities within African American communities, as well as the nation as a whole.

Statistics show that 25% of all entrepreneurs are females, and women start 30% of all businesses, compared to 75% of male entrepreneurs who start 70% of all businesses.[10] Small business owners support product innovation, job development, underserved areas, and America's financial stability. Therefore, small businesses are valuable assets to the American economy. Case in point: small businesses account for 99.9% of the 29.6 million firms conducting business in the United States.[11]

Small Business Matters

American entrepreneurs are contributors to the American economy and American culture.[10] Small businesses create 1.5 million jobs annually. Entrepreneurs are individuals who sell products or services to generate a profit. Small business owners create 64% of all new jobs. In 2015, small businesses accounted for 47.5% of private workforce employment in the United States.[12] According to the SBA, seven out of 10 new employer businesses survive at least two years, and about half of those new businesses survive five years. At the beginning of 2008, 627,200 businesses opened, and by the end of 2008, 595,600 firms closed. Business survival is not assured for any business owner.

American entrepreneurialism grew at an unprecedented rate from the mid-19th century through the 20th century.[13] Historically, entrepreneurialism in America created large corporations and big businesses throughout the United States. These large corporations had political, societal, and cultural influences.[14] Although a volatile occupation, entrepreneurialism continues to grow at unparalleled rates.

Business Failure Common

The idea of becoming *one's own boss* or millionaire is seductive, yet no one can promise entrepreneurial success[15]. The SBA (Small Business Administration) reports that half a million businesses start up each year. Still, half a million businesses may close their doors each year. Although not all business closures result from business failure, only half of the business start-ups make it to the 4th year in business.[11] Currently, no single business theory accurately explains why some businesses fail, and others do not. Capital, planning, professional advice, staffing, and education are a few variables that researchers consider crucial for business success.[16]

Entrepreneurs fit into two categories. The first category includes successful, educated entrepreneurial professionals, and the second category includes struggling small-business owners who have yet to make a profit from their businesses.[17] Unfortunately, business ownership often leads to failure, and small-business owners form the largest group of consumer bankruptcies.

Why Black Women Are Starting Their Own Companies

Unemployment in the private sector, the lack of job advancement, and limited education lead individuals to entrepreneurialism. Prejudice within the employment sector, including the lack of job advancement and increased levels of unemployment, often leads minority business owners down the path of self-employment. Business ownership offers an alternative to ethnic, immigrant, and minority persons historically marginalized and discriminated against by the American mainstream labor force.[18]

Business ownership creates individualism for these groups, allowing them to promote themselves to positions they may not typically achieve in corporate America. Many would-be entrepreneurs seek business ownership because they want freedom.[19] This freedom may include freedom from working for someone else and the independent creative freedom that comes with owning a company. The appeal of business ownership attracts African Americans in particular. The definition of entrepreneurial freedom for the African American entrepreneur may include freedom from having to "prove they are worthy of promotion" within the corporate workforce. Ironically, African Americans may still experience discrimination within their entrepreneurial ventures, which can work as a limitation for African American women in business. African American business owners may meet difficulty securing the financial and social capital necessary to run a successful company.[20] Prejudice within the public market sector also creates a necessity for minority business ownership. Historically, mainstream economies often neglected to meet the needs of minority consumers. This neglect allowed minority business owners to fulfill the needs of these subgroups by selling their products and services to minorities.[21]

Feminine Leadership

Throughout American culture, men have dominated the world of entrepreneurialism and leadership, as shown by theories like the Great Man Theory. Wherein a leader had to be a prestigious pillar within his community or the nation and a White male. These expectations or requirements historically kept women and minorities from achieving cultural leadership, much less entrepreneurship.

The Great Man Theory restricted women and minorities from working in a leadership capacity. Female and minority entrepreneurialism and leadership increased in the 21st century. Female entrepreneurs are setting up entrepreneurial ventures and advancing in organizational leadership positions.[22]

The growth of female entrepreneurialism has caught the attention of scholars, stirring interest in exploring female entrepreneurship. Exploring the female entrepreneurial culture has encouraged scholars to consider the difference between male and female entrepreneurs and their leadership styles. A noted distinction between male and female entrepreneurs is their motivation for becoming entrepreneurs. Female entrepreneurs, in general, migrate toward entrepreneurialism because of their desire to produce a better livelihood while integrating family life and business life. Men, on the contrary, become entrepreneurs to achieve status, growth, and wealth.[22]

Other fundamental differences between male and female leadership include entrepreneurial culture; women perceive the importance of female entrepreneurial support groups while setting up their businesses. Male entrepreneurs are loners, competitive, and less likely to seek entrepreneurial networks for support. Research has shown that female managers lead differently than male leaders.[23]

Compared to male leaders, female leaders excel in corporate social responsibility (CSR), where the focus is on humanitarian giving. Female leaders can possess the emotional intelligence needed to execute social responsibility ideas.[23] The leaders' concern for corporate social responsibility may encourage workers to see themselves as change agents. Thus, corporate social responsibility may help workers to achieve a sense of accomplishment far beyond a paycheck.

Women in leadership positions tend to nurture and fashion relationships with their employees, thus positively affecting organizational performance by directly reaching workers.[24] Female leaders tend to give power to their employees, are more amiable than men are, and are innate transformational leaders. The perspectives of both male and female entrepreneurs differ on statistical, fundamental, and leadership levels.

Globalization has increased the presence of woman executives; however, female leaders are still highly underrepresented compared to their male counterparts in global business operations. In 2006 there were only eight women CEOs leading global Fortune 500 companies. Five of those Fortune 500 companies originated in the United States. Female leaders are underemployed in America, but women can create opportunities to lead by establishing businesses.[25] Evidence shows that corporations with women in top managerial positions do better financially than companies that do not have women in leading positions. The lack of female entrepreneurs and female leaders in global business limits diversity, ultimately threatening the success of companies.

Female leaders (in general), naturally encompass transformational, contingent, and participative leadership styles. These leadership styles are influential in global operations.[24] Bromley and Kirscher-Bromley described transformational leadership as leaders who form relationships with their followers; leaders who make use of the transformational leadership model involve themselves with the development of their employees.[26] These authors also suggested that transformational leaders encourage their employees and treat them as valued team members within the organization. Transformational leaders motivate workers; they empower employees to reach their full potential. Managers who use transformational leadership theory influence their followers to become leaders themselves. A transformational leader encourages and creates work environments that nurture employees' growth. Transformational leaders desire to make a positive impact in the lives of their followers.

Contingency theory builds on the premise that no perfect leadership theories or models exist when leading people within an organization. External and internal factors determine the right leadership style. According to contingency theory, leadership style is subject to change, depending on the environment. Contingency theory leaders have an innate ability to change as the situation dictates. Contingency theorists assert that one leadership style, although enough, may not be proper for every situation. Contingency leaders are not predictable; they are unique because they are not limited to one set way of carrying out a goal or set of tasks.[27]

The participative leadership theory model uses a team approach to organizational development. Participative leaders consider the opinions of individuals within the organization, particularly the followers. Leaders who make use of this theory allow their followers to aid in some of the decision-making processes. Participative leaders are not authoritarian and do not consider their workers subordinate. Such leaders are members of their team. Participative leaders consider the opinions of their followers-yet the leaders have the final word. A global leader who uses participative leadership theory understands that he or she alone does not have the answers, nor does an organization thrive because of the leader alone. Global leaders can receive help from using participative leadership methodologies within their operations. Participative leaders treat the organization like one machine with many parts: each part aids in the advancement of the organization. They use the talents, gifts, and abilities of those within their organization.

Each of the models theorizing these styles conceptualizes a relationship in which managers encourage their employees. Werhane (2007) noted that "empowerment is almost a mantra for women in leadership positions" (p. 8). Transformational, contingent, and participative leadership styles are highly beneficial in a global marketplace when compared to some classic leader models. It's important for business owners to know their leadership style. Knowing and perfecting your leadership style, can help you lead your team effectively.

Feminine leadership studies have also shown that female managers and entrepreneurs are still overcoming challenges and stereotypes associated with ancient gender hierarchal systems.[28] Female leaders need the same support that male leaders need to manage successful global and nonglobal operations. Societal demands of women's roles also add to the complexity of being a female leader in a traditional male-occupied global environment. For female executives to succeed in the global market, they need external support from society and their families. Female leaders need help and internal support from entrepreneurial networks. As family roles in society continue to change, female leaders will need more assistance. Societal gender roles should not make women choose between their careers and their families. If proper support systems were in place, women might find it easier to balance family and career. Additionally, education of society as a whole may dispel misconceptions about women in leadership positions.

The African American Female Entrepreneurial Experience

There is a profound lack of scholarly research specifically related to the African American female business experience; we are *only* told that African American women are starting businesses, yet not enough information exists that explores their unique experiences.[29] Entrepreneurial research has tended to focus on White males. "Scholars analyzing trends in self-employment and small-firm ownership among African Americans have been profoundly polarized for nearly 40 years" (p. 5).[30] Female entrepreneurs are another subgroup receiving limited attention in scholarly studies.[31] Literature concerning female entrepreneurism does not focus on African American women entrepreneurs and their stories; instead, the literature on female entrepreneurs paint a homogenous picture of feminine entrepreneurship while indicating the unique struggles of African American female entrepreneurs.[7] The literature does not capture the African American female entrepreneurial experience, yet African American female entrepreneurs are starting businesses at rapid rates within the United States. African American women own 34% of all minority women-owned businesses in the United States.[32] A fact corroborated by the SBA report showing that one in 20 African American women own businesses.[1] African American women are more likely to start a business than White women. Yet, African American female entrepreneurs experience marginalized income earnings compared to their White female and male counterparts.[4] Many factors contribute to financial success, including time in business and the numbers of employees.[15] Soft skill factors that contribute to the success of female entrepreneurs include cultural knowledge, communication, and human relations skills. Equally essential factors include family support, language and geographic location, a strong customer base, and quality staff members. Equally important is the availability of finance, opportunity availability, and providing professional services. Finally, successful female entrepreneurs are persistent and have an entrepreneurial mindset.

African American Women Business Comparisons

African American female entrepreneurs display a more positive attitude toward entrepreneurial training courses than their White counterparts.[33] The entrepreneurial disadvantage explains African American entrepreneurs' gravitation toward training programs. Overall, minority entrepreneurs have less managerial experience compared to nonminority groups.[34] African American women also have less graduate-level schooling and entrepreneurial experience compared to White female business owners. Decreased managerial experience and education may lead to reduced human capital.

African American female entrepreneurs have less social capital overall than White women. White entrepreneurs have more social capital because of entrepreneurial experience and training. Thus, African American entrepreneurs need and value training to increase their social capital. African American female business owners believe that such training will lead to successful businesses.[33]

African American female entrepreneurs typically belong to informal entrepreneurial social networks, such as church organizations, while White female entrepreneurs typically belong to formal networks.[11] According to the Employee Policy Foundation, by 2030, women will occupy 56% of managerial and 46% professional positions. This occurrence will be likely because of women completing more undergrad degrees than men.[33] Professional and managerial job advances increase the need for diversity in the workplace. The increase of African American women having higher education levels may help African American women who are seeking managerial and professional positions. However, while these opportunities do exist for African American women, bias based on ethnicity and gender is still evident. Furthermore, African American women may experience duality bias because they are both female and African American.

Dual Discrimination Theory

Puryear developed a dual discrimination hypothesis and dual discrimination theory: Women and African Americans are excluded from typical White male sectors of entrepreneurship because of workforce prejudice and prejudice within the entrepreneurial field.[7] The dual discrimination theory also suggests that women and minorities, specifically African American women, have lower odds of entering and staying in entrepreneur sectors. White men dominate managerial advancement in the workforce and are more successful within entrepreneurial endeavors. Nontraditional entrepreneurial fields will not have an economic interest for minorities who may deal with prejudice. Research has found that women are a gender minority in entrepreneurial areas that are primarily occupied by men.[7] Women are less likely to enter nontraditional entrepreneurial fields because of prejudice. According to Smith-Hunter and Kapp (2009), native-born African and Asian employees were less likely to become entrepreneurs compared to Whites. The study also concluded that African Americans were less likely to maintain self-employment.[5]

Black Women Entrepreneurs in Other Countries

According to Chiloana and Mayhew, "entrepreneurialism is a cross-cultural phenomenon with culturally specific aspects, and to understand it, one will have to relate to factors that influence entrepreneurial behavior p. 3."[35] Socioeconomic individual characteristics and subjective feelings are examples of factors that influence entrepreneurial behavior. Socioeconomic factors may include education, age, fear of failure, and motivation. Two areas that influence female entrepreneurs are socioeconomic opportunities and work status. In South Africa and other third world countries, Black women, in particular, turn to informal or entrepreneurial means to produce wealth because of the limitations in job opportunity and social services within their country.[35] This behavior is not limited to Black women in South Africa. Black women in America embrace entrepreneurialism because of the lack of job advancement and opportunity.

11

In South Africa, the informal entrepreneurial sector does not require a license, making business ownership easily attainable. Entrepreneurialism may supply a reliable alternative to unemployment and reduce poverty. Similarly, African American female entrepreneurs in America consider entrepreneurialism as an avenue to promote themselves and produce wealth. In other countries of the world, where per capita income is higher, women pursue an education before entrepreneurism, and women in countries with limited income seek new business ventures as opportunities to survive economic hardships and to take care of their families. In middle-class nations, women pursue entrepreneurism for the same reasons as women in poorer countries.[35]

Women in poorer countries or those who live in areas that have fewer opportunities pursue entrepreneurism to survive. In contrast, American women, especially African American women, may pursue entrepreneurism to advance. Research has shown that entrepreneurs who have some secondary and tertiary educational backgrounds tend to fare well in entrepreneurial endeavors. In particular, entrepreneurs who have more education tend to have greater access to information and experience.[35] Entrepreneurs who have education and work experience will create entrepreneurial endeavors *because* of their experience, as opposed to creating entrepreneurial experiences *because* of the need to survive.[36]

Female entrepreneurs are more likely to network than their male counterparts.[36] Networking is critical for both male and female entrepreneurs because social networking may lead them to the tools, education, and support systems that aid in their business growth. On a global scale, female entrepreneurs face compounded difficulties, such as limited business opportunities, skills, and resources.[10] Entrepreneurial opportunities for women are fewer than opportunities are for men; therefore, male entrepreneurial activity is higher.

Industries We Dominate and Why

African American female entrepreneurs tend to set up businesses in areas of service and retail rather than in non-traditional areas such as mining[5] where

White male entrepreneurs dominate. African American women-owned businesses are still scarce in such areas, despite the increase in numbers over the years. Women, in general, face opposition when attempting to create entrepreneurial opportunities in venues dominated by males.[37] Nontraditional areas representing 5% or fewer of women-owned businesses include mining, construction, wholesale trade, agriculture, manufacturing, transportation, public utilities, and communication.[5]

Research has shown that there are reasons African American female entrepreneurs gravitate to the service and trade industries. Female entrepreneurs dominate areas such as real estate, insurance, finance, services, and retail trade. Biases have restricted both women and minorities from specific industries. One theory is that trade industries require minimal capital and overhead cost and service industries, in general, need less start-up capital than nontraditional businesses.[37]

Another reason that women are attracted to traditional businesses is that, typically, service and retail industries are historically women's favorite businesses. Service and retail businesses are often considered more suitable for the feminine gender because these types of companies are viewed as extensions of homemaking.[5] African American female entrepreneurs with limited finances can start-up traditional businesses using less money. African American women have historically held submissive and subservient roles within American society in general.[38] American history reveals the roles expected of African American women, and most depictions of African American women show them in servant positions. For years, American racist viewed African American women as the help, the house cleaners, the servants, the nanny to the owners' children, and the owner's mistress.[41] After slavery and its stigma, American society's perception of Black women did not shift immediately; America did not view African Americans as American citizens.[14]

African American women were at the bottom of America's hierarchy; they had fewer rights than African American men and White women.[39] American racist viewed African American women as servants. This fact may have had a strong influence on the women's choice of service industries. The service industries were an area within the entrepreneurial field in which African American women believed they could flourish. Such areas provided the opportunity to create businesses with little financial commitment in a field with which the women were familiar. Furthermore, service industries overall do not require technical skills. This background is another reason why women, in general, flock to such industries within the workforce and in entrepreneurial endeavors.[39]

In addition, established gender roles in America contributed to gender bias in the work and entrepreneurial worlds. Gender biases limited women to specific roles that were considered appropriate for them. Primarily domestic, these roles restricted women to human service and caretaking positions.[22] Men's particular roles, on the contrary, were outside of the house (nondomestic). Men's roles focused on hard labor. Venues that required technical skills to complete. Even today, women who experience discrimination in competing with male-dominated positions within the workforce, may also experience it within the male-dominated entrepreneurial fields.

Where You Came From: Black Business Pre- and Post-Civil War

A historical look at African American entrepreneurial history in America reveals that Black Americans owned businesses during the antebellum (pre-Civil War) era, as well as, after the Civil War. Before the Civil War, slavery, legal restrictions, and intolerant legislation stifled African American freemen and slaves, limiting antebellum Black business participation.[40] However, some antebellum Black entrepreneurs, such as millionaire William Leidesdorff, successfully took advantage of pre-Civil War business endeavors. Other antebellum African American entrepreneurs operated a variety of business endeavors, including manufacturing, transportation, self-hired bondsmen, and tradespeople.[41] After the antebellum period, African American entrepreneurs often set up businesses in the service industry, such as restaurants, beauty parlors, and small mom-and-pop stores.[41]

Racism, laws, and regulations in the northern and southern United States restricted and discouraged African American entrepreneurial growth and profitability. Free Black antebellum entrepreneurs ran marginal businesses making nominal profits. However, the determination they displayed while pursuing entrepreneurialism on "unfair grounds" was admirable. The financial crash of 1857 spurred racial hostility against Black business owners, particularly in the Saint Louis area; that racial hostility influenced a decline in African American entrepreneurs, more so than the financial crash of 1857.[14]

Early Entrepreneur Research

Some of the earliest accounts of African American business studies come from work done by W.E.B. Du Bois. In the late 1800s, W.E.B. Du Bois hosted conferences in Atlanta for Black business owners. During the conferences, Du Bois explored the economic and social problems within African American communities housing African American businesses. He distributed the information gleaned from the conferences in Atlanta to government and state officials who had the power to influence philanthropic policymaking within the urban business community.

The Negro in Business Conference of 1899 provided the first academic research of its kind that shed light on Black capitalism in America. In 1899, while at the Atlanta University Conference, Du Bois surveyed 1,500 African American business owners and coined the concept of "The Negro in Business." The analysis of African American business owners gathered from the conference in Atlanta also helped Du Bois create the concept of local Negro Businessmen Leagues. Much of the information derived from Du Bois' research created the definition of Black business and the definition of a Black businessperson—a meaning tied to the amount of capital that business owners invested in their companies.

According to Du Bois, successful business owners were those who had stock for sale and a minimum capital investment of 500 dollars. Du Bois' business conferences were also unique because of the quantifiable data collected through interviews with Black business merchants. This data was set up through third-party confirmations and helped researchers to gain a better understanding of African American business success. At the time, the methodology used by the U.S. Census Bureau often underreported African American business achievement.

Prominent African American leader Booker T. Washington convinced Du Bois to provide Washington with the survey results and contacts from the 1,500 African American business owners surveyed at the Atlanta University. Washington used the contact information to call the first national business league meeting. He realized the value of Black entrepreneurship after noticing the growing number of Black male and female businesses in the early 20th century. Washington used his influence to encourage Black business owners to work together.

Du Bois and Washington repeatedly held lectures before business leaders, civic organizers, and educators at the Philadelphia Divinity School in 1907. These lectures often gave a historical account of African Americans in business and discussed Black business economics.[38] In 1907, Washington wrote *The Negro in Business*. In this book, Washington stressed his view of using African American business ownership as a road to achieve racial equality for African Americans. Washington and his followers thought that Black business success qualified Blacks for self-government and American citizenship privileges. Washington's book also included accounts of successful African American entrepreneurs. The topic of Black Business grew in the 1900s. However, it was not the sole focus of academic scholarly writing.[14] Business scholars at that time were also interested in African American achievement as whole encyclopedias, dictionaries, and similar media documented these achievements; Black business was merely a subject within the text.

Nineteenth-century researchers tried to solidify Black business as a stand-alone topic. In 1909, Booker T. Washington's son-in-law, Sidney Pittman, started a business serial called *The Negro Business League Herald*. Other publications followed. Many of the publications identified Black business owners' progress but failed to recognize their struggles.[41] Racism in America proved a detriment to African American entrepreneurs in the 19th century.[42] Banks would not give loans to Black business owners, and segregation forced them to work within urban enclaves.[43] In the 19th century, African

American business owners struggled to maintain business growth while the lack of financial capital limited business expansion.[43] After the Civil War, the northern states experienced a vast increase in freed Blacks escaping the constraints of the South during the Great Migration. The Jim Crow era brought with it continued segregation limiting African Americans' access to success compared to Whites.[42] During the Jim Crow era, African Americans relied on their neighborhoods and created urban enclaves where they organized themselves in ghetto communities. Some Black business owners were successful, and despite what they did not have, some Black business owners contributed financially and socially to their communities.

African American entrepreneurs had to carve out a niche for themselves, even within the Black community, if they wanted their businesses to survive. African American leaders advocated the development of healthy African American societies, business owners, community church leaders, and professionals. Their communities also thrived from within and dedicated themselves to becoming self-sustaining. Business research during the late 19th century focused on Black-consumer buying power and African American business development. The Black church also played a crucial role in helping Black businesses to set up themselves.[42] Historically, some Black business owners depended on Black customers for survival.[19]

Black Owned Business Comparisons

Nascent entrepreneurism for African Americans is 50% higher than for Whites.[44] African Americans are more likely to start businesses than Whites, yet they are less likely to own firms.[4] That is to say, African Americans are more likely to strive for entrepreneurialism but less likely to become self-employed business owners than Whites are, creating a paradox in the literature.

African American female business owners experienced a higher credit rejection rate at 51% compared to other minority and nonminority female entrepreneurs. Compared to White female business owners, Black female entrepreneurs were 47% less likely to apply for credit from fear of rejection.[45]

Sullivan and McCracken gathered data about Black entrepreneur men and women compared to White entrepreneurs.[17] According to their research, Blacks were five times likely to own unincorporated businesses compared to White business owners. Incorporation offers several benefits to business owners. Incorporation legalizes businesses and supplies a form of legal protection for the business owners' personal assets. Incorporation often makes businesses official or recognizable within state or federal government databases. The lack of being incorporated can limit business owners' ability to raise capital. Limited legal resources and scarce capital may have been critical factors in the small growth rate of Black-owned businesses when compared to White-owned businesses.[46]

Statistics have shown that Black-owned businesses are less successful and, in general, are more likely to go out of business than White-owned businesses, because of the lack of human and financial capital[44]. The U.S. government created The American Recovery and Reinvestment Act (ARRA) of February 2009, out of an understanding that business owners needed its financial and legislative support to remain economically workable. The ARRA gave 800 billion dollars in tax relief to support small businesses; however, none of the provisions was significant to African American women-owned businesses. African American female business owners received 7% of the funds given to women business owners and less than 5% (about $40 million) of vendor funds from the ARRA. The lack of human and financial capital may account for the limited number of African American owned businesses and the higher exit rates of African American owned businesses, compared to White-owned businesses.[4] Possessing individual economic capital is not a guarantee of entrepreneurial success. The lack of capital is a motivator, and the reason some minorities and women become entrepreneurs. Capital is a useful tool for business growth. African American entrepreneurs, especially female entrepreneurs, tend to enter service industries that do not require substantial amounts of capital or have high business start-up costs; nevertheless, to achieve business growth, entrepreneurs may need financial capital.

Disparities in household incomes (Whites compared to African Americans) may also limit African American owned businesses from accessing financial capital. Entrepreneurs may use their household income for business start-up costs, for loan collateral, or to show net worth. The average income in African American households is less than one-tenth of the average income of White households.[20] Prior financial capital is also beneficial to entrepreneur success and longevity.[4]

Having education alone is not an indicator of entrepreneurial success; American history tells of wildly successful American entrepreneurs across all ethnic and gender lines who had a limited education. Research also has suggested that people with higher education are least likely to start businesses.[35] However, education may lead entrepreneurs to pursue entrepreneurial endeavors that require technical skills, or to fields that have increased potential to pay the entrepreneur well.

African American female business owners migrate toward businesses that do not require extensive education. Bates and Lofstrom found that firms with highly educated owners are less likely to close than other firms. Individuals who go into businesses with human capital have more significant potential for entrepreneurial success and longevity. Experience, education, and ability are examples of human capital.

Courage to Defy the Odds

In the 1900s, going into the world of entrepreneurism in America was a challenge for any person; however, racism in America compounded entrepreneurial challenges for African Americans.[14] Banks would not loan them funding for their businesses. Segregation also limited where Black businesses could operate, which stifled Black business growth into mainstream venues.[38] In addition, the lack of business education and professional guidance hindered African American entrepreneurs, who, in the 19th century, were from lower socioeconomic backgrounds. Restrictions on information and limited resources affected African American entrepreneurism. Despite assorted barriers, African American business advocates pushed Black-owned businesses to consider other avenues to secure business viability.[41] Some of those avenues stressed that business owners become more modern and efficient to mitigate the increased competition from chain stores and immigrant retailers infiltrating African American communities.[14]

From a historical viewpoint, American women did not have the same educational opportunities as men. Likewise, before 1948, African American women could not own property or conduct legal transactions.[38] Similarly, some of the opportunities awarded to White women did not apply to African American women. A point often overlooked is that some opportunities awarded to African American males did not extend to African American women.

These restrictions placed on women in general, and specifically African American women, may have influenced their self-esteem and feelings of worthiness to compete in entrepreneurial activity. African American women entrepreneurs may have lacked the confidence required to compete successfully in entrepreneurial endeavors; nevertheless, some women became entrepreneurs despite the odds against them.[35]

Part II: 5 Keys to Success

Forecasting Business Success

The ability to predict business success and failure could help women interested in pursuing entrepreneurial endeavors by giving alerts about potential shortcomings.[47] A correct prediction of business success or failure may advise stakeholders of business pitfalls before investing. Knowledge concerning which businesses have more significant potential for success and failure would also be of interest to entrepreneurs; business failures are costly for everyone vested in the business. For example, a business failure may lead to bankruptcy, which also affects communities.[48] Scholarly research about what entrepreneurial success is—often measures success from a business performance standpoint. However, identifying business success from business performance alone is challenging. Throughout business performance studies, business researchers have based performance on either subjective factors, which may include entrepreneurs' personality and managerial skills, or objective factors, which may consist of the entrepreneurs' sale returns. Some researchers argue that a universal definition of *business performance* cannot be achieved within the scope of small-business firms.[16] While researchers stress that financial returns on investment prove business performance, for the small business owner, financial performance does not automatically constitute business success. On the contrary, entrepreneurs may determine their business success based on their personal feelings. Thus, offering a much broader choice of performance expectations.

Lussier 15-Variable Tool and Success

The Lussier 15-variable tool analyzes business failure and success rates; based on 15 success and failure variables deemed important to achieving business success. Researchers have tested the model's validity in North America, Central Eastern Europe, and Chile. The Lussier model tested entrepreneurial responses based on what participants consider to be essential resources for their businesses. Whether the entrepreneur is a minority business owner represents a variable used within the Lussier model, and minority entrepreneurs are more likely to fail when compared to non-minorities.[16]

Fear of Success Theory

African American women may also hinder their promotion and success within business organizations[49] through fear of success and fear of seeming incompetent. Women tend to have a greater fear of success than men do. According to Horner, women fear success because they expect that success will lead to increased competitive pursuits against men, with negative consequences, specifically femininity loss and social rejection[53]. In another germinal study, Senchak and Wheeler tested both male and female business students and found the students had the same level of fear of success; however, female participants had a greater fear of incompetence.[50] Moreover, Tomkiewicz, Bass, and Vaicys noted that African American women seeking advancement in business careers experience difficulties, which may negatively cause undue pressure within their work environment.[51] An example may include organizations hiring African American women solely based on their ethnicity rather than their ability to perform a job well. This situation may cause feelings of incompetency in women who believe that the company hired them to fill the organization's numerical quota. This belief may cause undue pressure on African American women within the workplace. Even with such constraints, progressive African American women are more likely to be more successful than their peers in pursuing their career goals because of their willingness to take chances even if success is not promised.

Oh snap! I said something here, this is where the book gets really good, carry on.

Born for Success

Let us define success in general. Success is simply the achievement of a goal or idea or concept. I have always had an appetite for achieving success in all things. I was raised to be successful, a natural leader, and an enterprising person. My mother told me I was a leader and not a follower while I was still a toddler. Leadership, for me, means self-responsibility, of being in control of myself so that I can enjoy a successful life and lead others. The first person you must be successful at leading is yourself—otherwise, no one will follow you. My appetite for success was developed through various areas of my life, starting with education. In my family, mediocrity was never condoned. Certainly, achieving the average was not good enough when it came to anything academic. At home, my family expected excellence in all things.

I grew up within a household where I learned early that *my* success in life was contingent on *my* ability to lead *my-self* to success. It was up to me to produce the results that I wanted to see in every area of my life. This expectation excited me because I learned that I could, indeed, teach myself how to achieve my goals. And many times, I put this knowledge to the test throughout my life. Like when I taught myself *how to* study early in my academic journey. Learning how to study was a significant key to my success. It put the power in my hands because I knew I could teach myself concepts—by learning how to break down and assimilate information. I learned how to teach myself things I did not know. I remained on the Dean's List throughout college.

Consequently, I was one of my first teachers because I learned how to teach myself. This mastery led to my academic success and success in life in general. I learned early on how my mind worked and my preferred learning style. In the same way, I incorporated self-responsibility within other aspects of my life—to help me reach my goals. And so, I grew up attacking my goals and usually hitting the targets I set to accomplish. Success is living your best life; in other words, living a life that makes you proud. Living out your dreams to the fullest and not letting anyone stop you. I was encouraged early on to dream big. And now I am here to encourage you!

My Study Background

I am a researcher with a cultivated taste for exploring Black *history* and women's issues. In 2007, I wrote my Master Thesis on the history of Black hair culture. In 2012, while in my doctoral program, I started exploring the behaviors and traits that led to the success of companies. Why were Black women starting businesses? What were their thoughts on success and failure? The more I studied the literature concerning the topics of entrepreneurs within America, African American entrepreneur experience, woman entrepreneurs, and African American woman entrepreneurs—the more I became fascinated with the ideal mindset for business success.

In 2012 I was a part-time entrepreneur. I was dipping my toes deeper into the entrepreneurial water and experiencing the multiple failures and successes that come with stepping into the role of an entrepreneur. I considered myself a part-time entrepreneur because I was working multiple jobs when I started my very first companies. By 2012 I had been playing around in the world of business for 5 years, I didn't know what I was doing at that point, but I knew if I kept going, making adjustments, that I would eventually see real success. True business success in my early entrepreneurial path meant working exclusively for myself, paying myself, and sustaining myself. I have finally gotten to that level of success and beyond. In 2012, I was confident that I would find Black women to interview who were in successful businesses more than five years old. I used five years as a baseline because, according to the Small Business Administration, more than half the businesses fail within their first years of business, and most entrepreneurs are out of business by their fifth year.

How do strong businesses run by Black women survive? These owners faced the challenges of starting a company. Indeed, these women overcame the challenges of dual discrimination (suggested by literature) that might be experienced by women of color. Finally, there is an absence of Black women business owners' experiences told within the literature. What was the secret sauce? What type of fortitude did you need to succeed in-spite-of the odds? I wanted to expand on the 2008 research from Beth Anne Reaves, which explored the lived experiences of women entrepreneurs[31].

I set out on a mission to explore the perceived dynamics that female business owners considered essential in creating and continuing their business. What I learned were the stories of five unique women who shared their hearts and brilliant minds with me. Based on the stories and data extrapolated from my interview questions, I was able to find several reoccurring clusters and themes. My business ownership journey confirmed these themes and patterns.

In 2012, I conducted a study concerning success factors of African American women business owners. My purpose for completing the study was partly for my doctoral completion requirements. I started my research based on my desire to do an ethnographic study "or a study of a specific ethnicity" and their experiences within a business. What I found while conducting the research was astonishing and conflicting. Although African American women-owned businesses were showing growth in various areas of development (including business quantity, number of employees, and profit), their profits and business success (overall) were poor compared to other minority and nonminority business owners. No agreed-upon explanation for this phenomenon existed within the literature. There was also a huge hole in the literature concerning Black woman entrepreneurs. What was strange and didn't make sense was that Black women were starting businesses at rapid rates, and yet their experiences were not being captured. Adding to the conflict was the fact that the number of African American women-owned start-ups were increasing; however, studies showed a small number of actual African American female-owned firms. African American female entrepreneur research often painted an identical picture of African American woman entrepreneurs.

The Keys Revealed

I discovered the Keys when I interviewed five female Black business owners in 2012 and through my entrepreneur experience—which dates to 2007. The Keys came from an academic process that included transcribing notes and tape-recording interviews for data analysis. I used a phenomenological design within the study and followed something known as the "Moustakas' modification of the Van Kaam method" for analyzing[52] data. This means that I set out to study a phenomenon, and I used a reliable method to collect and extrapolate data. The phenomenon was that although Black women were starting businesses at rapid rates; they were not as successful as they could be—compared to their counterparts. And I was trying to figure out why. In this case, I was also wondering why no one was talking about this gap. The process I completed to conduct the research was indeed a process; I will spare you the details of the analysis here. However, if you are doing academic level research on this topic, I recommend reviewing my study in full[60]. The most interesting thing to me was to see the patterns within the data. Patterns, if any, become readily identifiable at some point within the clustering process when you analyze qualitative data. Once the researcher identifies the patterns, themes ultimately arise from the data analysis.

My research included in-depth interviews with African American female entrepreneurs who had owned their businesses for five years or more. The interviews took place over the phone and were tape-recorded. I asked them about their lived experiences of being an African American female entrepreneur with a business older than five years. What factors or themes of factors contributed to their success?

I asked questions about their backgrounds to obtain an understanding of their family background, educational, and business experiences. I also focused on their business reflections. Business reflection questions helped me to gather the business owners' perceptions of their leadership styles, the challenges of being a business owner, and the factors that they thought contributed to their success. I asked for their recommendations for others wanting to start a business to glean what these owners considered important in creating and maintaining a successful business. Finally, I asked demographic questions to clarify the participants' characteristics further and to help me classify information.

I used Weft® qualitative data software to analyze my information and color-code participants' responses based on keywords. Next, I clustered the keywords according to each participant's experience. Eventually, I developed textural descriptions from the keywords, clustered data, and verbatim participant responses. These textural descriptions led to emerging themes that I color-coded for further analysis. Finally, I analyzed each research question's emerging themes for the revelation of major themes. Major themes were those themes that were relevant to the study. Frequently reoccurring themes were cited as key themes within the data.

KEY 1: MINDSET

I discovered the power of the first key—mindset—by living life and experiencing its ups and downs. My mother taught me about attitude when she was homeless, living in California. My mother always has a positive attitude; when we were homeless, it was no different. In fact, I didn't know we were homeless because my mother always attracted people that opened their homes, shelters, and hotels for us. Yes, you heard me correctly. My mother was homeless in the 80s with me, her daughter in Compton, California. I was three years old at the time, and my mother was escaping a relationship with an abusive ex. And yet I remember my mother singing. My mother is the poster woman for gratitude and faith. During my experience of being homeless, I can remember walking a lot, singing, and staying from place to place for a bit. I was happy in rough times because my mother demonstrated happiness personified. People didn't believe she was homeless back in the day because her attitude said otherwise. I watched my mother go from homeless to eventually owning her first home on a part-time salary because of her mindset.

My mother's lessons: spoken and unspoken, taught me the value of the power of mindset. It's your attitude that determines your success before anything. The same is true for business owners. We have to get our minds right. What does that mean? That means that to be successful in business, we often have to heal the mental blockages we have about our success. We must know that we are *worthy* of success and that we *can* think big. We must understand that we can think outside of the box and that it's okay not to know how to expand your business. Asking for help is also part of developing a healthy mindset. The wrong mindset is the one that gets you trapped in a vicious cycle of victimhood or false pride. The mindsets of victimhood and false pride can also make you feel inadequate. Neither mindset is a successful business mindset.

All is connected, mind, body, and soul—your holistic self. What I've learned over the years is, if you are holistically bound to negativity, your business may suffer. If you are not mentally well, you may impede your business success. I am not referring to mental illness; I am referring to toxic thinking. Toxic thinking will stop your success in life, including your business. Your attitude decides everything. Webster defines *attitude* as *a settled way of thinking or feeling about someone or something, typically one that is reflected in one's behavior*[54]. Another word for attitude is *point of view*. The point of view that you choose determines your actions. The actions you choose can help build or destroy your business. This factor is the number one reason mindset is vital to entrepreneurs.

One of the first books I read that encouraged me to reflect on what I was thinking, and explore the concept of mindset, was Joyce Meyers' book, *Battlefield of the Mind*. Within the text, Meyers reveals the magic of shining the light of consciousness on your thoughts. In other words, see your thoughts. You are a conscious being seeing your thoughts. You are not your thoughts[55]. And yet we can choose to focus our thoughts on higher vibrational things. We can adjust our mindset by adjusting our perspectives and seeing the full picture. Therefore, the proper mindset is one that can see the whole picture, a mindset that slows down, able to view all angles.

The mindset of a business owner must be flexible and agile. A winner's attitude is critical if you want to have a chance at success. One cannot be successful and a victim at the same time. Again, that is a trap. You must pour into yourself. This action will help you develop a successful mindset. By pouring into yourself I mean, you must get to know who you are. Knowledge of yourself can lead to a proper mindset. The more you know about yourself, your strengths, weaknesses, opportunities, and threats, the more confidence you will develop. The more confidence that you have, the more you will start manifesting and attracting what you want in your life and your business. The less toxic your mindset, the better off your business will be. If your mindset is toxic, your business will be toxic. As the saying goes, "wherever the mind goes, the body will follow[58]," the same is true for business. Wherever your mind goes, your business will follow. If you believe you are a failure before you get a chance to get your business off the ground, your probability of business success is minimal. Your negative mindset can quickly sabotage your success.

Being an entrepreneur is challenging. There is no doubt about this fact. I've already mentioned the statistics which indicate that most businesses fail within the first year, and many don't make it to the five-year mark. Many would-be entrepreneurs close their doors no sooner than opening them because of the challenges that often come when you own a business. Challenges can be vast and may include stressors like growing and scaling your business or even dealing with an irate customer. Every business owner has issues that he or she may have to overcome regardless of their ethnicity, making mindset the most crucial factor for everyone. And mindset is especially important for developing as an African American woman business owner. You can learn all of the keys, and yet if you don't apply the first key within your mental framework (before you attempt to use the other keys), your business may still fail. Why? Because your attitude is your foundation. And if you build your business with a negative mental attitude, you may manifest negativity. Therefore, mindset is the number one key for business success.

A Conscious Mindset

A conscious mindset occurs when one learns to separate the thinking mind from presence. The thinking mind can be all over the place: while presence—just *is*. All human beings have both a thinking mind and a presence. Eckhart Tolle refers to this presence as *consciousness* or *awareness*[55]. Developing presence is helpful for the entrepreneur. It can help you get a grip on your mind and learn how to make your mind work for you—rather than feeling like your mind is in control of you. You can develop a presence in many ways. One way is through meditation, which we will explore later, within the mindset section.

This section explores what the right business mindset looks like, feels like, walks like, and acts like. In this section, we will consider the mindsets of champions and the mental strategies they use to win the game. Life is a game, and having a business is like playing a very strategic game. You must have fun, and you must know the rules to play the game well. Rule number one is mastering a positive mindset.

What is your mindset? Your mindset is the way you think about things and your state of belief. It's an established set of attitudes held by someone. Your mind is defined as "the element of a person that enables them to be aware of the world and their experiences, to think, and to feel, the faculty of consciousness and thought."[53] I will add that your mindset is your *attitude* about a thing.

The keyword is attitude. What kind of attitude do you have, goddess? A conscious mind is one that is aware of itself. You are aware of what you are projecting. You are aware of the energy you are putting out. This attitude can attract people to your business opportunity. Your attitude is what helps drive your business success. How you perceive challenges, for example, is essential to your business success. It's quite normal for all entrepreneurs and people in general to experience both highs and lows. If you fall into the trap of "woe is me" with every challenge that comes your way, if you give up on your business idea before you honestly give yourself a chance— you may regret it later. You can avoid this kind of failure by checking your attitude and working on improving it. The proper business attitude can enhance your perception or mindset.

A successful business owner works to develop their mindset. What I have discovered (while working for myself) is that business ownership forces you to grow from deep within if you want to be successful. I think this growth primarily occurs because you must rely on yourself and sometimes your Highest Self, or God— if you believe in that—as I do. What I am saying is: sometimes, the shit hits the fan in your business, you are all alone, or you feel alone. Some tasks you may handle alone and other tasks you *must* handle alone.

Business ownership often involves you going deep within yourself to solve your challenges. You are your boss, the one writing your checks, the one cashing those checks, and the one paying the taxes! Business ownership plays on your confidence because often, events push you into situations that you didn't foresee. Like the one time I had an unexpected business expense to the tune of $14K automatically deducted from my business account. The proper mindset kept me from sinking. I had energy for creating a plan to replace the funds immediately. A productive mindset keeps you from permanently abandoning ship. Sure, you may curse, spit in the dirt, and question your sanity for starting a business. However, a conscious business owner will pull strength out of the ethers, get a grip, and get back to business. Business ownership stretches you and can help you grow as an individual. To succeed and go far in business—you must allow your business to improve you. You must be willing to improve the way you think. Before you can improve, it's essential to evaluate your mindset. You must become conscious or aware of your mind first to evaluate it.

You must become aware of the state of your mind. Is your mind busy? Is your mind telling you negative thoughts? You may find that as you awaken and start evaluating your thoughts that there are lies and other toxic things. You may have been telling yourself lies about yourself, your situation, or another's situation. What is your mind thinking about on a daily basis?

How does this thinking hinder or help your business success? Are your thoughts leading to sales? Or are your thoughts full of defeat? Becoming conscious is like turning on the lights in your mind and looking at what you've been feeding yourself. Becoming aware is an opportunity to clean the house in your mind. You may discover by observing your conscious mind that your subconscious mind holds patterns in its depths. Your subconscious mind is the part of the mind which you are not fully aware of, but which influences your actions and feelings.[53]

Compared to your conscious mind, which is responsible for logic and reasoning, your subconscious mind is the part responsible for your involuntary actions. We develop patterns in our subconscious. Some of these patterns are not beneficial, and some patterns are beneficial. When you become conscious, you become aware of these patterns. You also become aware that you are not your mind.

Once you start watching your mind *think* daily, you will see thoughts come and go; you will realize that you *and* your mind are *not* necessarily the same. In other words, *you* are not your thoughts. Consciousness means that you start thinking (reflecting) about what you're thinking about; you become aware of your thoughts. This awareness creates freedom because you are no longer weighed down and stressed out by every thought and emotion that you witness your body experiencing. Instead, you allow yourself to feel the emotion without judgment—you simply observe. The conscious being is who you are. You separate your thoughts from your person and separate your emotions from yourself.

A conscious business owner allows herself to *feel*; you are not a robot. An aware business owner is one who feels their feelings profoundly and allows for emotions to be as they are without judgment. Emotion is energy moving through the body. You can observe emotions and feel the energy. Don't run from feelings. Become aware of—not controlled—by your emotions and thoughts. Realize that you are more profound than your emotions and thoughts. Know that you are beyond your mind.

You can also decode and reprogram your subconscious mind. This action creates peace. And peace is what can give you the gasoline to move forward on some of your worst business days. The more peaceful your mindset, the better off you are for health and sanity reasons. There is great peace in knowing that you are not your mind. Therefore, you do not have to get absorbed into everything that it says. You must learn how to step outside of yourself and the chaos of your mind and emotions. Underneath the chaos, a conscious business owner is grounded. They are in touch with that part of themselves that's unmovable and unshakable. Grounding is what keeps you from running. It's your consciousness that grounds you. Grounding helps you keep a panoramic view of yourself and your company.

A conscious business owner is someone aware of who they are. The first step to consciousness is self-awareness. Self-awareness is what keeps you from envy and jealousy. It keeps you from comparing yourself to others. Once you know who you are and the greatness you have, you will not need anything on the outside to confirm who you are. You may have people who inspire you and that you admire, yet you will know your power, and the greatness you have. Once you know what you came here to do, discover yourself doing it, and you know why you are doing it, then you will know what creative talents you possess. You will no longer feel threatened by anyone. The only person you compete with is yourself. Because there is no one else like you, we are each beautiful and unique in our own ways. You must know what makes you unique as a business owner and an individual.

A business owner who knows who they are finds it easy to celebrate the success of others. You must know who you are. You must understand your assets: critical components for business growth and success. Are you familiar with a SWOT analysis? A SWOT analysis is immensely useful for organizations. The SWOT analysis helps the organization determine where they are strong and where they need to improve and what tools they have. The SWOT analysis consists of strengths, weaknesses, opportunities, and threats. A business owner must know all these things about themselves and the business they provide. This awareness is part of learning to become conscious and developing your business mindset.

Know Thyself—Free Thyself

Self-awareness is also crucial because knowing who you are will help you develop perseverance. The more information you have written down about yourself (hint, SWOT analysis homework assignment), the more you know what gifts or tools you have available to you. You can also see what tools you want to develop. A full toolkit of reliable resources that you can use when the going gets tough increases your chance of becoming a successful entrepreneur. For example, one of my gifts is love; I have a heart that forgives fast. I consider this to be an asset. As a business owner, I have experienced countless disappointments: sometimes, from people I trusted and called a friend. Had I not activated my natural gift of love from deep down from beyond my heart chakra, I would be miserable, cynical and wouldn't trust a soul. I have used the gift of love to forgive a multitude of wrongs, and my mindset has taught me to know that all things work for my good. This awareness has kept me in business.

My success emerges from my mindset. I began to awaken: to study myself. I got in touch with my inner thoughts and read self-help books. Then I considered my family; I explored where I came from, my roots, my bloodline, and my ancestors. I went all the way in, and I studied the Kabbalah, astrology and numerology, alchemy, and many other esoteric concepts. I did this to, "Know Thyself." Next, I started studying consciousness itself and the levels of consciousness, as discussed in Ken Keyes's book, *Handbook of Consciousness*. The more I studied esoteric concepts, the more I began to know myself; the more my confidence grew. I started to connect my heart to my company.

The more you know yourself, the more you trust yourself as a business owner. You know your capabilities. Sometimes as a business owner, you may have to make choices based on your gut. You may have all the reason in the world to say yes, yet, your gut may tell you no. Trusting yourself is not always easy, or popular, yet it can lead to favorable outcomes. Like the one time, I had to push the production of a course project to meet a tight deadline, only to sell $25K of courses in one hour and $60K in one week. Had I not trusted my gut and listened to my team, the project would not have been completed and ready to sell! The lack of consciousness can cause you not to trust yourself or to listen to your gut. You are not aware. Therefore, a successful business owner starts with awakening their consciousness. A conscious business owner is a present business owner. They are aware.

Not only are they aware, but a conscious business owner is in control of themselves. They exude peace because external circumstances do not sway them, nor do their own thoughts derail them. Consciousness is the intro to mindset because all enormously successful things start from presence. It's this awareness that shines the light on consciousness. And when you are fully present, you can see things from a big lens; you can see the ramifications of your actions before acting.

An Accountable Mindset

One of the best books I read is called the *Power of Personal Accountability*, by Mark Samuel and Sophie Chiche. Accountability is what lights the fire underneath you. It pushes you on days when you would rather give up! It's your Self-coach. On the days that I wanted to put forth little effort, I encouraged myself! Sometimes that's what you have to do, and that's called accountability. You must pick yourself up because sometimes there will only be you. The world will disappoint you at times. The people of the world can also bless you.

Accountability teaches you how to be the captain of your fate and not fall into the trap of being a victim. I've taken the concept of accountability a tad farther; I believe that you can ultimately create the life and business you want regardless of your circumstances. It may not be easy, but it can be done, and once again: mindset helps. As a business owner, you must adopt excellent thinking; you cannot afford to think in an average way. You must learn how to expect fucking more for yourself! You cannot afford to be a victim, because victimhood will exhaust you and leave you with no energy to accomplish your goals. Victimhood will defeat you before you get started by attracting things and experiences to you that you don't want or need. And the more you become a victim mentally, the more bullshit you will physically attract into your life. If you think the world is always against you, then the world will undoubtedly appear to be your enemy. And if you continue to see yourself as less than (name your limiter), you will be treated as such. You can be aware of the madness you may experience from others and not be consumed by it. Again, you must "know thyself," as we discussed earlier.

Accountability is about taking control of your destiny, even in impossible circumstances. The only thing that keeps you from your destiny—is you. The only thing that pushes you to your destiny—is you. How? You can manifest the life that you want despite the unfairness or disparities that you may experience. The chances are that you will interact with challenging people and obstacles along your entrepreneurial journey. Your path may be full of both blessings and challenges. Yet you are not responsible for unconscious people that treat you like crap because of your skinsuit. Not personally taking what others say keeps toxic crap from sticking to you. You can return it to the sender. Otherwise, you will easily find yourself becoming offended and defeated if you make negativity your focus. The wonderful thing about working for yourself is that you can choose whom you give your products or services to and you can go where you are wanted and welcomed. You cannot change the behavior of others, but you can control your outcome.

You can affect change behind the scenes by making your voice known and creating change. I asked African American female business owners if "As a female business owner, did they think they faced challenges perhaps not faced by male business owners?" I also asked them, "if as an African American female business owner, did they think they faced challenges not faced by White business owners?" If this was true, I wanted to know what those challenges were. My series of questions intended to find the similarities in challenges respondents considered unique in their experience of being African American female business owners. The majority of the women interviewed, 80% of the respondents (four out of five), agreed that they faced challenges precisely because of their female gender. Most respondents, 80% (four out of five), also agreed that they faced difficulties because of their African American race. Is this true? It was true for the women I interviewed. Not every African American female entrepreneur has the exact same story. Yet, the women in my research study confirmed the statistic that suggests that African American female business owners may face challenges because of their gender and ethnicity.

There are ways to deal with prejudice. It is essential as a business owner that you aim to think and act strategically and professionally when faced with challenging circumstances. For example, where you feel someone has discriminated against you. Some of the challenges you experience may be extreme and require you to pursue legal action. For instance, in cases of discrimination, or if we're wrongly accused or slandered by a customer because of our ethnicity.

In the mindset of someone with poor thinking, being an African American female entrepreneur ought to be the last thing on earth to do. You already have two strikes against you: One, you are melanated, and two, you are a woman. So, what's a girl to do? Give up on her dream of running her company? Absolutely not. There are many successful African American female entrepreneurs; we have discussed successful African American entrepreneurs throughout this book. Not everyone is going to want to do business with you. Yet if you always assume that they don't or care that it's because of your melanin or gender, and you let that be your focus, then you will never reach your goals. Sometimes it may be true; sometimes, it may not be true. Either way, if it's nothing that requires action that can lead to a resolution, then leave it alone. Let a fool be a fool, don't get wrapped up in the offense. If you do, you will be so busy focusing on who rejected your offer, that you might miss your next opportunity. In business, you don't want to take anything personally for too long because it may add stress, and you may feel defeated. It's okay to feel sad, but the point is to rise again.

In my experience, entrepreneurship has been anything but easy. I am not sure if it would be easier if I were another color or gender: I doubt it. I've seen male and female entrepreneurs from all nationalities achieve both success and failure. I've witnessed my fellow entrepreneurs put countless hours and energy into their business. Some of them achieved success, and some of them didn't. Ethnicity and gender are not in itself indicators of success. If it were, then all White men who start businesses would be successful. This expectation is certainly not the case. In my experience, being an African American woman within certain industries has neither helped nor hindered my success. I never allowed it to. This lack of hindrance is primarily because of my perspective.

I overcome negativity by working smarter than my business competition. I don't see myself as less than, I remind myself of my strengths and focus on my goals. I see my melanin and femininity as an asset, not a liability, and so it serves me. There have certainly been occasions throughout my entrepreneurial path where I felt unheard, undervalued, and dismissed. Sometimes these situations were mostly due to male chauvinism. In my early cannabis days, I worked around lots of older men. It felt like a *man's world*, reminiscent of my police officer days because most of my coworkers were men, a male-dominated work culture.

Early on, I had to deal with narrow-mindedness. If I were treated better as an employee, I would have never branched out on my own. I would not be writing this book now if I had always been treated well. I would not be an entrepreneur. I am grateful! I didn't always get the respect my ego wanted; I had to get over my ego. People can be rude and ignorant. It's part of human nature and no excuse. Other people's ignorance is not your issue. What I am saying is that you are not accountable for how people treat you; you *are* accountable for what you do with that information and your life path. You *are* responsible if you let someone else kill your dreams. You will kick yourself later if you allow people to control your life.

I overcome the naysayers by pushing myself onward and targeting my audience—people who want to hear from me—specifically, women. I have a worthy goal to carry out within my business, and I focus on that, and I talk to the people who I want to serve within my industry. I focus on their wants and needs. I keep my focus away from people who don't believe or prejudge me and focus on serving people who love my services. You can be aware of the disparities experienced by African American female entrepreneurs and worst-case scenarios and still succeed. You can even experience heartless bias and prosper like those that came before you. Some of our ancestors had less and did more! Don't let your challenging experiences overwhelm you so-much-so that you give-up before you start. Or just give up altogether! Don't assume that being a successful entrepreneur is not in your favor. That's insane! You can help so many people with your products and/or services. There's an entire world out there, and it needs you! In all your uniqueness. It needs your thoughts and ideas. The world needs the things that only you can do. You came here to create.

Not everyone will appreciate your art, yet the right eyes will see you. There are going to be people that accept you and people that reject you. You must start looking at your melanin as an asset and not a liability. You are also beyond your skinsuit. Beyond the title of Black Women. You are a Being, stardust! Science proves that all humans contain cosmic dust within their DNA. You want to learn how to play up your assets. You can't allow the statistics to frighten you from achieving your dreams. Some internet opportunities are helping to level the playing field. In 2020 you can succeed regardless of your appearance. You can achieve your dreams despite the limited thinking of the people around you. Don't allow a few bad experiences to keep you from your destiny!

You want to focus on the opportunities that you will attract to yourself, and you will attract more good things. You want to do business where you are wanted and develop the reserve you may need to deal with the naysayers. There will always be naysayers and those who may treat you as an inferior being, and it may or may not have anything to do with your gender or skin tone. The thing is, how other people view you is not your business. And therefore, you don't give a fuck. Why? Because you are too busy and determined, creating your own destiny, and you are accountable to yourself. They must be accountable to themselves. People who mistreat others because of the other person's appearance are mentally ill and cannot see that we are the same. It's not your issue to help them to see the light. Your goal is to do your best and focus on building and minding your business. Accountability helps you to handle yourself; it does not require you to take on someone else's emotions. What a relief! Accountability forces you to believe in yourself and what you can do. It keeps your focus on what matters, so you don't waste energy.

A Persistent Mind

Remaining persistent regardless of the obstacles was a core theme discovered from interviews with African American female business owners. Staying persistent is a mindset principle. All the participants in 2012 spoke passionately about the importance of African American women business owners being strong, confident, determined, and persistent, regardless of the obstacles. Participants encouraged future African American female entrepreneurs to be assertive and almost unapologetic in their quest to pursue their aims of entrepreneurial freedom. Be unapologetic. Indeed, you owe yourself success. You will not always be sweet and gentle on this journey. Assertiveness is required if you want to play the entrepreneur game and win it! You can't be afraid or consumed in how others view you. The most important feeling to be aware of is how you feel about yourself. It's better to accept all parts of you, including your shadow side, the side that you think you need to fix. What matters is that your conscience is clear, and you can sleep well at night. If you sleep well at night, then keep moving forward, goddess. Stay true to your own convictions. If you are not sleeping at night, and you don't have a health concern, evaluate your conscience.

Persistence requires determination to see a goal through. It will require persistence to make your entrepreneur dreams a reality; you can't be afraid of offending people. Your success may offend some and inspire others. As you grow as a business owner, you focus on making your customers happy; a happy customer generates sales. The only people you strive to please is your customer; everyone else can take a number. Know in advance that you can't please everyone all the time. Don't apologize for being your authentic self; how people choose to label you is their prerogative. A persistent mind does not let the opinions of others or anything else keep them from attaining their dreams. Persistence encourages focus so that you can achieve whatever you set out to accomplish. It does not matter how many roadblocks persistence endures; it will keep pushing.

Do you know how many daily roadblocks you encounter running your own company? Many. Not only that, but you may be responsible for finding solutions for those roadblocks. If you want to continue your path of business ownership, you go through the roadblocks. Within the cannabis industry, for example, there are many roadblocks. Even opening a business bank account and applying for a merchant account is often not a straightforward process and can prove to be challenging. The cannabis industry is ripe with issues that I've learned to overcome. I got so good at maneuvering through the cannabis space that I created a course on how I did it to cut peoples' learning curve. If I would've allowed roadblocks to stop me from moving forward, I would not have found solutions to my problems and created courses to share those solutions. If I never had any roadblocks, I would not have any content for my courses. Your mess can become your message; persistence allows for growth where you thought there was no life! One of my favorite sayings is, this too shall pass. It means all things good, bad, and indifferent end. Trouble does not always last. If you stay persistent long enough and make decisions, eventually, your success will unfold. All entrepreneurs benefit from adding a dose of persistence to their confidence arsenal. Persistence to keep going becomes even more critical if you experience prejudice while running a business, this is an observation borne by the statements of the participants I analyzed[60].

...Some potential customers don't want to let African Americans in their houses (White customers sometimes have a lack of trust of Black business owners). I have had difficulty selling my products because I can't gain access to their homes. When I sell Mary Kay cosmetics, I have to have the right contact person in order to be granted access into White customers' homes. (R04)

...I have recently been fortunate a 30-day grace period to pay for printing. As an African American female business owner, I often have to pay right then and there; there is no grace period. (R05)

The importance of remaining persistent regardless of the obstacles encountered was supported by my research study where I asked participants why they achieved success. Participants stressed the importance of identifying and pursuing their wants, no matter the cost. Business ownership was something they wanted for varied reasons; in some cases, they pursued it without strong family support. Nevertheless, they pursued it relentlessly. R04 stated, "I was determined; I did not give up. ...they told me to find one thing and stick to that, but I figured that God gave me a lot of talent, and I was going to use it."

When you are determined to use your talents, you will. We each have talents. Some of our talents can help people and bring us wealth. In this situation everyone benefits, by helping people we help ourselves. Someone wants your product and/or service, so you sell it in exchange for payment. When you help yourself and live out your dreams, you support and inspire others. Without persistence, you may give up before you reach your first sale. With perseverance, you are inspiring others, whether you know it or not. What you see as a small success is an enormous success to someone else.

Even deciding to start a company requires a mind shift and is a huge step. Staying the course is even rarer. Most businesses fail. Most companies don't see their first profit for years. I didn't sell one cup of tea or coffee with my first drop shipping company in 2007; I had zero sales. Fast forward to 2017, I started my second drop shipping company and reached over

$5K in sales within a month! If it weren't for being persistent, I wouldn't have seen that success and much more. Tenacity in business helped me to create products and services that took me from $0 to over $20K a month. Persistence made me willing to try drop shipping again. I didn't let my past failure keep me from drop shipping. This time, I drop shipped CBD, not tea or coffee. Now, I teach my clients how they can dropship and make money while they sleep, with little or no overhead. Persistence helps you troubleshoot and see what needs to be adjusted to achieve an outcome. Persistence is a supervisor and a teacher.

You can't give up. Why? If you give up too soon, you'll never know how great you could become. You'll never get to see the type of long-lasting impact you can make should you decide to give up. You can't quit, not when you've made up in your mind to pursue your wants no matter the costs. Your dream must be bigger than you! You must remember what brought you to the place of wanting to be an entrepreneur. It's not about what your mother wants for you or what your friends want for you. Owning a business is about taking control of your life and making something happen with your own abilities. You use a lot of your own strength (especially in the beginning) to accomplish your goals. This need for control can make entrepreneurship a lonely reality. It's a journey you truly do take mostly by yourself, even if you have people in your life. This journey may be especially lonely for African American female entrepreneurs who are often single and must rely on themselves. You can also have people around you and yet still feel isolated as an entrepreneur unless your friends are also entrepreneurs. Sometimes you simply aren't speaking the same language as the people around you. I was prepared for loneness because school and work isolated me. I can remember early on in my entrepreneurial career; it was extremely challenging because I struggled alone. I struggled, and yet I was determined to do more because I was tired of struggling. When I refer to struggling, I am referring to handling every part of your business alone, or just about alone.

My budget to farm out work was limited. Like many melanated women, I was juggling six things, including my home life, a fulltime career, and a part-time job as a college professor. It was exhausting, to say the least. I did all the customer service work myself, in the evening, after working my 9 to 5 job. I had to be very strategic with my marketing. I needed to have my market dialed-in and advertise in the right magazines and media outlets. I didn't know what my cost to acquire customers was back then, but I know it had to be low because my budget was limited. I can remember when I held my first conference for one of my earlier companies. I had just launched my company, and I was planning to hold a conference at an upscale hotel in downtown Milwaukee. I used every resource I had to pull the conference together, including my family and friends, to help wherever they could. My early days of learning how to work miracles is a nod to the determination required to succeed.

Four out of five (80%) of the respondents studied were single and divorced; several participants expressed the lack of family support they received while pursuing their entrepreneurial endeavors[60]. As expressed by R04, "You'd be surprised how many family members told me not to be an entrepreneur. African American people are brainwashed; it takes a while to change their slave mentality." You don't become an entrepreneur so that you become a socialite unless that is your business. On the contrary, you spend many days and nights working on your business. Sacrificing your friends and sometimes even your family and yourself because you have a goal.

Entrepreneurs take risks, and some of us are not encouraged to take risks by people close to us. It's their fear that makes them discourage you, and this same fear may keep them stagnant. Sometimes your loved ones may feel that what's good enough for them is also good enough for you, not realizing you have your own dreams. If you allow that toxic energy to infiltrate your life, it may make you stagnant as well. Negative people will weaken your ability to succeed. You would be better alone than to be with someone that drains you. We talk about the topic of family in the fifth key.

The theme of remaining persistent regardless of obstacles encountered emerged when I asked African American female entrepreneurs to identify the resources that they used to start their businesses. Business owners, in general, may not have all the tools they need to be successful. However, according to the data identified, successful African American female entrepreneurs are those who persisted beyond real or imagined shortcomings[60]. African American women who want to become successful business owners must pursue that desire relentlessly, using the resources they have at their disposal. As noted by R02,

> I used the resources that I had. I did not have a lot of funds to go buy things, but I was determined to make it work. It was professional. It's funny thinking about it now, but I made it work.

You must remain persistent if you want to reach your goals. Persistence doesn't always feel good. Persistence sometimes feels like work, because that's what's required—old fashioned work. Effort can be fun too! Work is not a dirty word. It may also suck. We don't see a lot of work online. We see the results of the work.

Online we see people's Instagram pictures of their business success; we see the new cars and new penthouses. We love showing the best parts of the business. We love showing the fruits of our labor. But we don't like showing the actual labor and the struggle. We like showing the beginning and end of the movie, but like Bishop T.D. Jakes said in one of his sermons, "We don't know what to do with the hellacious middle[59]."

We don't tell people about the entrepreneurial process, and when we do, we sugarcoat it. We don't like telling people how we had to borrow money from our friends to pay for our rent last month while we were waiting to get paid by clients. We don't like telling people about the business deal that we hoped for-that fell through at the last second. We don't tell people how lonely and tired we are and that we cried ourselves to sleep the night before. Why is that? Because we have fallen into the illusion that perfection has more value than real business experiences, both good and bad.

We don't value failure; we are embarrassed by it. We don't see that failure is a positive platform that helps us launch into success. What the illusion doesn't tell us is that the pendulum swings, your entrepreneur path is full of highs and lows. Therefore, you can't afford to give up! Success is just as much in your reach as failure is! Success will require persistence from any and everyone who dares to take such an exciting risk! This reality is all the truer for African American women entrepreneurs who may face unique challenges.

In your opinion, what are the characteristics of a successful African American female entrepreneur?

I asked participants to identify the characteristics of a successful African American entrepreneur. The answer provided by R01 coincided with the core theme of remaining persistent regardless of the obstacles. The participant simply stated, "African American female entrepreneurs must know the challenges, but not let those challenges discourage them."

Although the participants noted racial and gender bias as a challenge for African American female business owners to overcome, the overall mindset was on remaining persistent regardless of the obstacles. I also had to be persistent when my first company failed. I failed because my energy was scattered in several directions. I had to have enough drive to pick myself off the floor and try again. I was determined to work for myself. Like many other African American female entrepreneurs, being fed-up within the workplace is what led me down the path of running my own company. As previously mentioned, I was the Queen of jobs. Yet the satisfaction I received from working for someone was waning although I had what some would consider "good" jobs.

I never felt like I was getting paid enough for my passion. It took persistence to be bold enough to cut myself free from the security of having a government job. After 12 years of working for the government, I cut myself free because the vision of where I wanted to be superseded where I was. There had to be more out there. I was right! There is so much more to life than working a 9 to 5 job for someone else. Persistence to succeed despite the odds is a huge piece of the formula I used to break free. Persistence is what drives me within my companies today. It is part of the energy I am using to dedicate myself to writing this book. I am determined to reach you, educate you, and give you the tools on how to be a successful entrepreneur. Without persistence, when you are faced with challenges, you may give up before the breakthrough happens.

After starting several companies, trying different things, and failing, and finally finding my sweet spot, I can attest to the power of mindset, specifically persistence. Boy, can I attest to this! I feel like I want to testify. I had to be persistent when I was working multiple jobs while going to school for my Doctorate and starting a tea and coffee company. In fact, it took persistence to start my first company in 2007. I can remember attending my first entrepreneur seminar. I was motivated to attend. My electricity had recently been abruptly cut off because of an unexpected bill and missed payment. I had so many jobs, including a government job, and I was still (almost) living paycheck-to-paycheck like most Americans. I was taking care of myself and my household. I was in too deep financially. I had no room in my budget for unexpected emergencies. I was taking care of most things financially by myself. Although I had retirement savings and a Roth IRA, I was under financial duress. I was ready for something different. Looking at the bright side, I took the invitation to open an online store as a sign from the Goddess. Plus, I was tired of eating bean burritos (the business seminar offered a free dinner).

In my analysis, I asked participants what advice they would give to an African American woman desiring to start a business. One participant shared: "I would tell them to continue to be strong and to keep the passion. They should focus on what they love about themselves and keep going forward." Another participant responded,

> As African American women, we put ourselves last a lot, but in business, you have to know what you want and go after it. I would tell them to not be afraid to be concerned with themselves. They have to know what they want and go after it.

You must think creatively and adopt what I call crazy faith if you want to be a successful entrepreneur. You must learn how to see past the situation and the circumstance, the difficulty, and sometimes the unfairness. The fact remains that life is not fair, and sometimes things stay the same for a long time. What you can control is the way you think about it. You can make the change first by realizing that you are more than capable of manifesting the life you want. You can become an alchemist by learning how to turn lemons into lemonade. As a determined business owner, you learn how to make the most out of your challenging situations. Persistence helps you push forward. When interviewed, African American female business owners mentioned the importance of taking ownership. Taking control of your business and your mind is essential. A persistent mindset is one that hits the target, come hell, or high water! Willpower is the battery (energy) that you must have to see your way through and out of challenging situations experienced by business owners. Pushing through is even more critical for people who often have fewer tangible resources. An African American woman must learn to self-motivate herself as a business owner. She must be persistent in being her own cheerleader. Persistence inspires business owners to be creative in overcoming challenges.

A Positive Mindset

It was the winter of 2011, and it was a frigidly cold and very typical day in Wisconsin. In 2011 I was working for the government. I had been working for the government for 11 years at that point. I was also working part-time for a couple of colleges. In addition to that, I was working periodically as a brand ambassador, and I had the audacity to start a dance fitness class as a side business. I was doing all these things while going to school full-time in the doctoral program. I didn't want to keep working like I was, yet I had goals. In the winter of 2011, on that very cold day in Wisconsin, I was looking for a positive word. Let's be honest; the reason I had to motivate myself is that I was tired of working for someone else and playing their game by their rules. I needed to hear a message of remaining positive in the face of seeming disaster and impossible and unsavory circumstances.

I was overwhelmed with the stuff of life. I needed something to keep me motivated. Books are a huge part of my stress relief arsenal. Books kept me going on days my energy was running on empty. I'd fallen in love with audiobooks; I'd decided to take advantage of my travel time and listen to motivational books while driving to work. I was always a fan of Napoleon Hills' work in *Think and Grow Rich*. At the time, I was using his 17-step formula for success to advance in all areas of my life and, specifically, to complete my doctoral degree.

The concept of positive mental attitude was introduced in 1937 by Napoleon Hill in his book *Think and Grow Rich*. I felt like I was stuck between a rock and a hard place because I wanted to be free and become my own boss. I wanted to finish my doctorate. Plus, I wanted my companies to supply financial freedom for me. I was pushing myself beyond the brink. Beyond the stress barrier, I was introduced to the concept before listening to the audiobook, *Success Through a Positive Mental Attitude*, by Napoleon Hill and Clement Stone. On that day, while listening to the audiobook, on my way to work, the message of Positive Mental Attitude was loud and clear. "P.M.A stands for Positive Mental Attitude," that's what the author said. And we must decide to be positive. Just like we can choose to be negative. That doesn't imply that we should walk around with fake plastic smiles while we're hurting. It does suggest that even though seemingly undesirable things may happen to you, it's your perspective about what is happening that matters the most. Positive thinking, when applied to business, is one of the secret ingredients to your success as an entrepreneur. Over the years, I've had to learn how to master my thoughts so that I could control the stress that often comes from owning a company.

How PMA Helps Business Owners

Positive thinking can help you solve problems better and with less stress. Challenges will occur when running your business. PMA keeps you from turning a challenge into a problem. Problems can swiftly raise your stress levels, whereas challenges, though sometimes hard, are manageable and easier to get through. Challenges feel doable for me, while problems feel like doom and gloom. Challenges keep you sharp. Problems can quickly wear you down. Again, it's how you think about the situation and not the situation itself-that is the true wisdom to be gleaned here.

Positive thinking helps you to solve problems from a calm vantage point and a clear perspective. Perspective is the key to solving the struggles you will endure on your entrepreneurial journey. Perspective is like being able to see things from outside of your body. As a business owner, it's a skill that can help you in your most stressful moments. In my personal experience, it kept me from jumping to conclusions and making business decisions exclusively on emotions.

Perspective grounds you, it allows you to have a time-out. And for me, perspective kept me from giving up every time things got tough for me. Like the time I had offers to buy a company I created, and my business partner didn't share the same vision. Or like the time I was down to my last few hundred products, and my manufacturer was barely responsive. Since then, the only partner I work with is my romantic partner, and I have long since left my manufacturer. Yet, my point is, had I not had the right perspective in those stressful situations, I would not have given my business the chance to grow through the hard times. The right perspective, for me, means always being able to see the full picture and the ability to see the outcome. The most important thing for me is viewing things from an optimistic mindset and keeping peace within my soul no matter what the situation looks like on the surface. This discipline helps me win the *battle of the mind.*

Your PMA can give you the energy to deal with an often-demanding field. The less energy we burn up in being negative, the more energy we have to create the life and business we want. That's why I never understood why people waste their energy holding on to the dead past or the imagined future. When you do that, you are ignoring the power of this very moment. Your energy is elsewhere. If your energy is scattered, how quickly do you think your business will fall apart. Yes, there absolutely is a connection between your energy and the success of your business. If you are continually burning up your energy holding on to grudges, you may be blind to the next offer. Or worse, holding onto the past and your disappointment, may prevent you from attracting the next opportunity. Your business runs off of your energy. Especially in those early years, when your staff might be slim or unreliable, a common issue for business owners, especially African American women[38]

A PMA can create a chain reaction within your surroundings. Have you ever heard someone give a good belly laugh and then smiled, yourself?

Have you ever shot your thoughts across a room with a look? Or watched a business meeting of people turn deadly silent when the big boss storms through? That's energy moving. Your thoughts are unseen things, but you *are not* these things. You are not your thoughts, and yet your thoughts untamed give rise to emotions, and emotions are energy. Energy does not have to be seen to be felt. You can damage a person with your eyes or choose to send love with your smile. The reaction from the body can often come from your thoughts, feelings, and emotions. Positive thinking can set off a chain reaction within your body, which sometimes leads to action. Negative thinking can affect the energy of other people and spread like an infectious disease. When I worked for the government, I worked within a profoundly serious department. Clothing with any type of wild pattern was frowned upon, and laugher had to be kept to a minimum. This place was not the police department, but an office environment. It felt like, what I bet Fort Knox feels like—cold.

Positive thoughts can improve your confidence in yourself and your ability to lead and sell. This is because when you think positive, you feel positive, and when you feel positive, you radiate happiness. If you feel good, you will perform better. Why? Because of science. When you feel good, you release feel-good endorphins within your body. These endorphins may help boost your mood and self-esteem. It can even give you energy and put an extra pep in your step. When I feel a positive emotion, it makes me want to reach out and share it. When you feel good, it shows, and you attract people. This attraction is especially handy if you are doing a tradeshow for your company, and you need to attract people to your booth. Tradeshows are an awesome way to promote your brand and lead to a sale. There are techniques that you can use to have a successful tradeshow. A successful tradeshow starts the moment you decide to take part in a tradeshow. You want to carry that positive attitude with you wherever you go because people will want to hear what you have to say. You want the opportunity to communicate with your customers face-to-face. If you keep a positive attitude, your customers will respond to your energy. Remember, like attracts like.

Black Girl Magic and Confidence

There is something authentic about Black girl magic. I think this is true for any being that feels or has been trained to feel less than others. And African American women have been told that story over and over. How many times are we told: no one thinks we are attractive, so we develop low self-esteem? We are not all of anything. First of all, although we share similarities, we *each* have our own voice. Second, *we* don't have anything to prove. Third, people love the diversity found in African looks. Do you know how big Africa is? Africa is actually three times bigger than the United States. Africa is the mother of all Human beings.

It's time to let go of any victim consciousness if we are going to be successful with our businesses and expand. You cannot be hugely successful and stuck in a victim state of mind. It's time for us to expand and truly see our greatness and areas where we can collectively grow. You develop a stronger sense of self by discovering who you are as an individual and a business owner. It's imperative that you build your self-esteem so that your confidence strengthens, and you can deal with the rejection that all business owners experience.

Adjusting your mindset is a process. This adjustment may not happen overnight. This is a daily task. Holy scripture suggests that you renew your mind daily. Every day there is work to do. We must expand our beliefs. It took me a long time to know that I had nothing to prove to anyone. I still get that message daily. And the freedom I find from embracing that truth is amazing. That's why I can tell you in advance that no one is less than or more than you. You are unique. No one is superior to you. Nor are you superior to them. This fact is what I want African American women to know. There is nothing for an African American woman to prove to anyone, except herself. This fact is what she must know. The first step to having a successful business is adopting the right attitude.

Accountability creates confidence; that's yet another reason it's essential to develop this side of your mindset. Confidence is vital in every aspect of your business. The more confidence you have and can display, the more you can draw things and business opportunities to you. The more confidence you have, the more you will show your ability, and people will have no choice but to take you seriously because your talents will shine. I've seen this within my own path. I let my desire to be heard as a business owner push me to the forefront and to success. I've demonstrated this through my success at tradeshows by selling and marketing my CBD brand. I also made myself available for speaking engagements at CBD friendly tradeshows. I didn't hear a "yes" every time I gave my sales pitch. But I grew up knowing that "delayed does not mean denied." When someone told me "no," I did not allow myself to become offended, defeated, in short, to become a victim.

Instead, I heard "not right now." "Not right now" is not a defeat. Accountability gives me confidence. Because I am determined, I believe in myself; it starts with believing in yourself. I use confidence to overcome obstacles. You cannot maximize your success without confidence. You are selling a product and/or service. It helps if you believe in what you are selling. Because others will believe too, then they will buy it.

When I started my first CBD company, I was selling CBD products to distributors. Confidence is what helped me close deals and get distributers to sell my products. If I had not had confidence in my skills or abilities, then I wouldn't bother to be a business owner, especially in high-reward and high-risk industries, such as the cannabis industry. The more I overcame challenges, the more my confidence grew. The concept of always having to prove themselves as serious business owners because of their gender also came up during my research. A lack of confidence was shared and cited as a challenge by women business owners. The fear of being dominated by male employees was also cited as a unique challenge experienced by female business owners.

> I definitely do think we as women face challenges. I don't know if it has something to do with us having confidence and not being sure of how to handle things within a business. When doing (business) with my male counterparts, I have to always prove myself. You have to prove that you are a businessperson and that you're professional. I think we are different; we are not on the same plane as our male counterparts, and I think that's for a variety of reasons. (R04)

I've felt this on occasion within the cannabis industry. Although this field has more women in executive positions than any other industry, there will always be people that judge the book by its cover. I've learned to laugh things off. And not take things seriously unless there is a legal need.

Nothing that people do can change who you are or what you've experienced, regardless of how they treat you. You can learn to use positive and so-called negative experiences as fuel to motivate you. Even if people are negative, you can use the experience for your growth. Success is the best revenge. Success is connecting to your target audience, the people you want to talk to, and reach, with love and service. Remember, as you are getting your business out there, people don't know you. Some will judge you and misjudge you. Let your superior services speak to those you want to do business with; your professionalism will prove you worthy. Your offerings will bring clients to you. Successful people solve problems or help people solve their challenges. We each want good service in exchange for our money. People who assume you cannot be of service to them solely because of your ethnicity and gender are the ones that miss out on how you could improve their lives. But you don't care because you focus on whom you can serve. Again, you can be specific about your target audience and speak in their voice regardless of your appearance. Your target audience may be from all ethnicities. People who judge skin tone exclusively are also exceedingly rare, so don't waste your energy being consumed by a few rotten apples.

Don't let past pain and experience from an unconscious person turn you into the judgmental being you despise. Keep your focus on winning. Continue to build yourself, and your self-esteem will develop so much that rejection will not ruin you. All business owners, in general, have to gain the customer's trust to win their business. It also depends on the industry you choose. If you select an industry predominately dominated by men, such as construction, then you may encounter outdated thinking. You will also meet people who welcome and embrace the diversity within the industry. Most people won't care either way about your looks. And folks who doubt you in the beginning, for whatever reason, can be won over through excellent service. Don't be afraid of going into industries that interest you but are dominated by men. Be creative, enhance a service that exists. Study the industry you intend to enter, find a mentor, and network. I cover networking and its importance later in the book. Some people are limited in their thinking and judge others on trivial matters.

> I think the biggest challenge I have is being taken seriously. I don't have too many males that work within my company because I am afraid of them becoming domineering. I have a lot of females that work for me. I now have a couple of males on my board, but I have had the past experience of men not taking me seriously and trying to take over my business. (R05)

Letting your services speak for themselves is enough, goddess. Don't let fear from past experiences consume you and keep you from working with all people. The reality of the situation is that you can't please everyone every time no matter what you do, and assholes come in all varieties. Proving oneself as a serious business owner was also revealed as a challenge for African American female entrepreneurs;

> Definitely, there are lots of obstacles in our path along the way that we experience as females and as Black female business owners. The issue of racism, there is an issue of not being taken seriously in business as a female, especially as a young female business owner. Again, not being taken seriously is one of the challenges for African American women.

Another woman said,

> African American female business owners should not let anyone intimidate them. Some men and races within the same gender tend to get intimidated when you're an African American woman who has her own business and confident at the same time. African American women should not let anyone discourage them from being a confident business owner.

I agree. Let no one discourage you from becoming the confident business owner that you know you are. Use the keys within this book to build the confidence required to have a successful company. The fact is—all entrepreneurs, if they are in business long enough, will have business situations that will challenge their self-esteem. Challenges, like keeping the accounting straight affect many of us. By the way, please hire an accountant as soon as you have a budget, unless that is your specialty. There will be many days when you may not feel good enough or even qualified to run your business. Those days will come and go. Some days you will also feel like you are on top of the world. This, too, shall pass. Being an entrepreneur is all about overcoming the difficulties for everyone that chooses this path. The longer you stay in business and stay committed to the process of running a business, the more mistakes you have the chance of making. The more mistakes you make, the closer to success you can get. If you learn as you go, mistakes mean movement; you are doing something. It takes action to do anything. Mistakes also help you develop new useful business tools, like mindset, and therefore help you build your confidence. After you have survived failure, you will not be afraid of it.

Five Ways to Cultivate a Healthy Mindset

1. **Focus on the power of the present moment.** Prevent your mind from ruminating over the past and worrying about the future. Eckhart Tolle is one of my favorite teachers. In his teachings, he helps you to focus on your *now*. By narrowing your focus to exactly what's happening at that very moment of your life situation, you can see clearly. Seeing clearly helps you make better decisions. Often, we feel anxiety, stress, or other unpleasant emotions as business owners because our minds wander out of the present. We might be worried about meeting a project deadline or past issues with a fulfillment shipping company.

It is no secret that entrepreneurs also experience unpleasant situations in their now moments. What Tolle, and teachers like him, suggest is that by focusing exclusively on the now, you bring presence (attention) to any situation. I have discovered repeatedly that often the situation is never as bad as I imagined and that most things offer a resolution. It's your presence, which you can find in stillness, that gives you the wisdom to recognize the resolution if you need to find one. Perhaps, a resolution is not even required. As a business owner, staying in the present moment helps you to conserve your energy and look at your business from an aerial view. The aerial view is what gives you clarity. Clarity is what's required to create a vision for your company, and it also drives your business success. Improve your vision by opening your eyes and widening your view of the now.

2. **Take inventory by counting your blessings**. After you have focused your attention on the present moment, count your blessings. Often, it is not until we fix our mind on our now moments that we realize (or are open to) the beauty that surrounds us, even as chaos engulfs us. Placing your energy in all the things you are grateful for helps open the door to abundance. I suggest you make a list of the things you are grateful for and repeat this list aloud to yourself. If you don't have a piece of paper and a pen, your voice alone, professing your gratitude can shift your entire vibration. Shifting your vibration may be precisely what your business needs to get out of a rut and close the next deal.

When you begin to focus on what you already have, you encourage an atmosphere of gratitude that surrounds you and helps you keep your peace. Not to mention, you attract more abundance. This attraction occurs because like energy is attracted to like energy, and we tend to attract more of what we are focused on. Therefore, you might have solely focused on that one contract that you didn't secure. Next, you placed all of your energy into hoping that you didn't lose another contract opportunity, only to keep attracting failed contract opportunities. The more you focus on losing, the more you make losing part of your reality. The more you focus on what you have already won, the more you win. Focusing on what you have, transforms your thoughts, and can make you smile even on the darkest days of building your business. Plus, when you take inventory of what you have, you can easily see where you can make improvements to your company and yourself.

3. **Don't simply think positively, act positively!** Positive thinking is more than a notion; it's an action. You want your positive thinking

to lead to positive doing in all aspects of your business. You want to put things into action and personify your passion. In other words, you feel so good as an individual that it has a trickle-down effect on your business. And people you do business with enjoy you. People you encounter love to be in your presence because you make them feel good by how you treat them. You make them feel good because your energy is high, and every contact you make feels your high energy. Positive action puts you on the path of implementing positive change. Business owners go through a lot of trial and error, often graduating from the school of hard knocks.

Shifting my mind to positive thinking in any unsavory situation has been pertinent to my success because the shift often leads to positive action. There were times as a business owner when the only comfort I had was my belief that everything would turn out well. Sometimes there wasn't any evidence that I would survive the world of business, and yet it was my positive attitude that encouraged me to continue. My belief helped to shift my reality. My positive mindset opened doors that I could not have seen if I was stuck in a funk. Repeated positive action helps you build momentum.

4. **Surround yourself with positive people**. The more positive that you become, the more you will attract positive people and experiences into your life. The more positive people you add to your life, the better you will feel. As you shine from the inside out with joy, you want to remain mindful about who shares your space. Birds of a feather do flock together. You don't want to surround yourself with people who are negative because their vibration and attitude can rub off on you. Negative people will drain you of your most valuable resource—your energy.

On the contrary, positive people create a forcefield of positive energy around you. Positive people pour into your cup and add value to your atmosphere. Positive people are magnets for positive experiences because that's what they attract. Positive people are assets. They help to keep you lifted up, which is especially helpful during challenging times. In my early

CBD industry days, I hired a young lady to assist me with social media posting on Facebook. Every time I came in contact with this young lady at the office, she was happy and smiling. It wasn't as if she was forcing it; she naturally had a kind and light disposition. She reduced my stress load by displaying an awesome attitude while handling my company's social media brand. She gave me peace because she saved me time. I could focus my energy elsewhere, and she brought me joy because she never complained. Positive people are a joy to work beside! They can lower your stress levels!

5. **Accept crappy and happy days equally.** I like to add balance to everything I teach. Positive thinking doesn't mean that everything always is peachy keen. It does not mean that you walk around with your head in the clouds. Adjusting your mindset to see situations in an unattached way teaches you how to accept both the acceptable and the unacceptable. This statement means you accept with equal equanimity the good and bad times that you will face within your company. Learn to not be *so quick* to label things as good or bad and consider it all experience.

Running a business is full of surprises; you have to adopt a mindset of serenity to maintain your peace. It is healing and honest to remind yourself that all things come to an end. It is never too late to re-chart your course. Surrendering to the acceptable and the unacceptable, accepting what is, is what Eckhart Tolle would term, "saying 'yes' to the present moment[55]"—an internal yes. This acceptance does not mean you cannot act on the external reality if the situation calls for action, and the situation may indeed call for action.

An internal *yes* is accepting the moment as it shows up in your reality because it IS in your reality. The premise is that to reject your present moment is actual madness because the present moment is here in whatever shape it takes. Even if you don't like the shape of the present moment, (and you may not), to deny the present moment by refusing to accept it does not change the present's reality. The only way to change something is to act. Even non-action is acting because you're deciding not to act.

To know what action to take as a business owner, you must have a clear mindset. Accepting the present moment (as it is) helps you to cultivate a mindset of presence, which will serve you well when you need to make essential business decisions. Accepting that happy and crappy days represent a Divine surrender. Acceptance will help you cut through the chaos and see a solution if one exists. I feel like my entire path of being an entrepreneur has been littered with Divine surrender. To be on this journey literally means to go with the flow. You become magical as an entrepreneur when you become flexible. Business flexibility is developed by mentally bending, stretching, and pulling in various directions. Your muscles are developed throughout your business, as you learn how to go with the flow, open to what being a business owner brings you on any given day. You learn how to become a true alchemist and turn lemons into lemonade.

Some of my best business breakthroughs would not have happened without the proper mindset. Each piece is essential. Consciousness, accountability, persistence, and positive thinking all pave the road to success, and they each work together. For example, consciousness to start a business is what led me to the exploration of working for myself. Accountability to myself gave me the courage to leave my job and led me to my first investor. Persistence gives me the wherewithal to continue despite the ups and downs of business. A positive mindset is what keeps my heart open to all of the possibilities around me. My research identified mindset as a crucial ingredient to entrepreneurial success; my experience as a business owner confirms the validity and truth of this fact. I've also discovered, as an entrepreneur, that there is much more to success than mindset.

Key 2: Defining Success Your Own Way

If you want a clear picture of where you are going-you must visualize exactly where you *want* to be. You visualize the outcome. The outcome is what success looks like to you. I learned this technique from one of my first business coaches. He asked me one *Question*.

Where do you see yourself in five years if neither time nor money was no obstacle?

This question brings the business owner to a place of envisioning what success looks like for them, which is especially critical to business success. This realization leads us to our 2nd key.

Defining Success Your Way

As an entrepreneur, you get to define success using your terms. For some business owners, success means being able to work from home and spend time with their families. According to research by Reaves (2008), female entrepreneurs overall have a different perception of success when compared to their male counterparts[54]. Women, in general, are motivated to become entrepreneurs because of their desire to merge family and business life while producing a better livelihood. Men, on the contrary, desire status, growth, and wealth from their entrepreneurial endeavors[55]. Women who merge family and business life while keeping their customers satisfied consider themselves successful[31]. Other factors such as receiving positive client and peer feedback, client satisfaction, overcoming gender and race discrimination, and achieving self-sufficiency through entrepreneurialism were identified as strong measures of success among the participants[60].

I wanted to be free from my 9 to 5 career. I was strongly motivated to work for myself. I took my success in steps. My first success was researching business opportunities. My second success was deciding the best way to enter the world of business. My third success was starting my first company. You see a pattern. Every step I took towards working for myself counted as a success because every step got me closer to my goal of working exclusively for myself.

Success comes for the business owner that sets goals. If you are carrying out the goals that you created for yourself, then you are successful. Success is what you define success to be. In my research study, one participant noted, "Good feedback from my peers and my clients are important; those are my measurements of success." For me, success is making other people successful within their businesses. Testimonials from paying clients never get old! I found that helping my clients make money and helping people is my sweet spot. I measure my success based on my abilities to teach people about what I do. I duplicate my success by helping others succeed. When people follow my formula and achieve success, it translates as *Goal Accomplished* and a victory for me. I genuinely rejoice when my clients rejoice—this is another way that I measure achievement. Knowing that my service works is huge. Witnessing concrete success (manifest in the businesses of the customers you have consulted)-is a blessing.

A good reputation is essential. The theme of having different perceptions of success emerged from my research study. A participant shared, "Successful female entrepreneurs are ferocious; they do not let people tell them, it that it can't be done; they overcome and try it anyway." I agree. The fact that you put yourself out there and take risks is admirable for anyone, especially people who are constantly told it couldn't be done. A successful entrepreneur is a person who defies the odds and does things their way. They take risks. You automatically take a chance by stepping into the ring. An African American female entrepreneur may consider herself successful because she treads outside of the box, (despite the odds), to start a company with limited resources, in the first place. Every step forward and every small victory count as a success.

Increased financial wealth was not listed as a primary indicator of success[60]. In fact, the majority of interviewees shared the same viewpoint. When asked about the characteristics of successful African American female entrepreneurs, a participant said, "If you satisfy your customers or clients, then you are successful; it is not about the money." It's not *all* about the money. Financial performance, for the business owner in general, does not automatically translate as entrepreneurial success; the perception of success varies for each business owner (Garrett-Scott, 2009).[14] Financial performance is not an automatic indicator of success. Yet, financial freedom is just as critical to me as personal freedom. In my world, they go together.

Money is important! It's what's required to live within this dimension. Money is not evil. Money is energy. It is neither good nor bad. Money can help you expand your business or compete with less struggle because you have access to more resources. It's time to start thinking big and expand your definition of financial wealth. You make money in business by selling. The more you sell, the more attractive you are to investors. I witnessed this; one of my first CBD companies received offers from investors looking to buy it out within six months of launching. These offers were for $500K! The companies would not have made offers if there were no sales on the books. And the amount the investors offer is often based on your company's sales.

Without sales, you have no company. Therefore, money matters. Clients are what drive the sale. Without customers, there is no one to serve. You have no business. If your customers are not happy-then, what is the point of your wealth? Within this journey, I've met millionaires and billionaires that couldn't sleep at night. Yes, they were making a lot of money, but they treated everyone around them like crap. They were toxic and driven by money rather than people. They lacked balance. They burned bridges wherever they went. Their customers suffered, and these millionaires and billionaires suffered too. I learned by watching people receive their karma. If you mistreat your customers eventually, you will lose them. If you happen to get rich manipulating people, eventually you will pay for it. You might even pay with your health. These observations are why my motto is the one that I learned in the Air Force: *Integrity first, Service before self, Excellence in all I do.* This motto is what I use as a measurement of my success.

Success, for me, means living the life you want, and this includes not having to choose between family and business. You can have a family *and* run a successful business. Freedom is what attracts me to running a business. For the longest time, I wanted to work from home. I eventually started teaching online, and it demanded much of my time for little pay. Yet, working remotely in academia gave me my first experience of working from the comfort of my living room in my PJs. It taught me that it was possible (for me) to work from home, lead effectively, and get things done in different time zones. I got a boost in confidence. I've been working from home for myself now for a little over four years. Only this time, I choose what to pay myself. And I charge my worth. I have made more money working from home within a month than I have ever made working in a year for someone else! That includes my federal job. I've had far more success working for myself than I've ever had when I worked for someone else, even on my worst days.

Women entrepreneurs overall have different measures of success. Yet what's not known about our entrepreneurial experiences is why some of us have different measures of success. The answer may or may not be complicated. Or, the answer may lead to discoveries that help us create longer-lasting businesses. People measure success in diverse ways based on so many variables. This situation reminds me of a PBS show I saw once where the show was comparing the retirement of African American people to the retirement of White people. The African American people in the study were glad they survived the stress of work and *lived to see* retirement. That accomplishment was the celebration itself, compared to the White people within the study who were celebrating their retirement *and* celebrating their new retirement lives. There is no right or wrong way to define business success. The key is: you must determine what success looks like to you as a business owner. You start discovering what success looks like for you by defining what you want.

Know Your Wants and Whys

What do you want and why are you here? You must know *why* you are adamant about being an entrepreneur in the first place. Otherwise, why bother to be persistent in a challenging endeavor? You must know what you want as an entrepreneur. Next, go deeper and *know why* you want what you seek. For example, you are pursuing money to provide you with a lifestyle of freedom. What does freedom look like for you? Or is your dream to open a school in another country? What is your first country, and why?

The businesses that were the most successful for me, were the businesses that had a strong sense of *why* attached—identifying your *why* is like identifying the driving force behind your passion. By naming your *why* you fuel your persistence. The first question I ask all my clients is what brings them to their industry. The reason I ask this question is to encourage them to start the process of finding their *why*. Your *why* is what helps you to develop your vision.

Identifying your *why* is powerful for three reasons. **First, it gives your company depth and deeper meaning.** Making a lot of money is a fantastic goal to have, and yet there are so many more reasons to become an entrepreneur. Having a business allows an African American woman to reach and connect to the rest of the world; it's our contribution. Brainstorming about how you want to help and add to the culture of this world will take you beyond "just making some money." Brainstorming will force you to think about the bigger picture and the lives you can affect simply by being a compassionate business owner and yourself.

Second, it will force you to think beyond the box and beyond your perceived limitations. Your *why* is where you create your vision for the world. When you connect your heart to your business, and you look to make a difference in the lives of others, then the universe will support you. **Third, connecting with your heart and making a difference in the lives of others may help your business resonate with other people**, which leads to lifelong customers, beyond sales. The reason that companies with meaning resonate with customers is that customers like to feel like they are part of something bigger than themselves. They want win-win situations. Millennials, for example, prefer to purchase products from companies that give back. In every company I've launched, I've made it a goal to give back. When I started my first CBD company, for every CBD product that customers purchased, I gave 100 mg of CBD to children with epilepsy. I've not had one complaint from one customer, and the testimonials from those who received the oil never get old. I also had a free *CBD Success Course* giveback program, where I offered free courses to high school seniors, in some of the roughest areas in Chicago.

I gave back to select charter schools that poured compassion into the lives of the youth they encountered. We empowered the faculty by giving them an exciting course to teach, which showed their students how to get into America's number one 2020 industry. Teaching this course could indeed enrich their students' lives. We educated the students through our eight-week course. Then we connected them to our trusted, vetted professionals to assist the students with the elements required to start a successful CBD brand, like marketing, for example. When my business partner announced to our private and public Facebook group about our giveback program, the announcement garnered so much support. Professionals within our groups offered their services for free to the youth within the charter schools. There is an outpouring of love within our community. Create a community of love.

People from all shades, sexes, and creeds enjoy giving back. Creating a network of people who love giving back is unstoppable. People with hearts know how good their heart feels when they can make a difference. Some people find their purpose through your passion. Give them a cause to support. Not all people are not divided, or racist. That is a misconception. If you speak your brand message clearly, the right ears will hear you, the right eyes will see you. If you love giving back and you make that part of your brand, you will attract others with the same heart. Giving back can grant a wish or prayer for someone. Love is the frequency I prefer, and it shows within each business that I create. Love is the very root of why I do anything.

Making money alone may not be enough for you to keep going, yet a cause that pulls on your heartstrings will motivate you daily. Your business is *more than* about you, *having a business*, for the sake of having a business, or being a self-proclaimed "Boss." As an entrepreneur, you also can become an international change agent. The keys in this book, combined with your will, intelligence, training, and application, may help you compete globally. Bosses look for ways they can create other bosses and multiply their generosity. They do this by giving back. Giving back is what opens the door to abundance. It's one thing to create a product. It's another thing to lead an entire industry and become a strong voice. That's what I experienced once I identified *what* I wanted and *why* I wanted it.

Within any industry you choose, you are going to experience the challenges of being an entrepreneur. I can assure you that there are going to be days when you NEED a reason to get out of bed. This need is especially true on days you feel defeated. I always experience my *why* pushing me forward, even as I type this paragraph. Business is about so much more than what we think. I like to imagine that my business is bigger than me. My business is a goddess business. I am fueled by something that exceeds me; I am driven by humanity. I've always been. I learn from each new business that I start and experience. I was already familiar with the power of writing my vision down in 2016 when I entered the cannabis industry. Upon arrival, I'd discovered that it was time to rewrite my *why* statement for this new industry. My previous company was a holistic health company for women. I still wanted to work with women. What was my reason for wanting to be in this new space? Why did I want to be in the cannabis industry? The cannabis industry was brand new to me then. I had to write the statement down and put my words in a place where I could see them daily.

When I wrote my *why* statement, I was far from my goal, and yet I wrote it with passion because I was determined to achieve it. I can remember it like it was yesterday because I wrote my *why* statement while working as a manager of a dispensary. Although I'd broken free from traditional employment, when I started a career in cannabis and ultimately became a cannabis entrepreneur, I started at the bottom. I worked many jobs, trimming flowers, packing pre-rolls, delivering cannabis, managing budtenders, and creating policies for dispensaries. No one cared that I had a doctorate when I managed my first dispensary. I even cleaned the toilets. I earned my stripes, and I dealt with a lot of bullshit in my early cannabis days. If I didn't have my *why* written out...honey! There is no way I would've endured some of my early challenges, like dealing with male chauvinism, managing employees, and working endless shifts as a budtender.

When I initially started in the cannabis industry, my goal was to "become the highest-paid and most sought after woman in the cannabis industry…." I set a goal to be an expert within the industry…I visualized myself creating products, services, and ideas that helped mankind (especially women) live better brighter and richer lives with cannabis. I set a visualization statement having no idea what I was going to create. At the time I wrote the statement, I was working as a manager at a dispensary that I helped launch. I wrote my statement before I knew I was going to lead the CBD industry. I wrote it when I knew in my soul that I had what it took to create a successful company because the dispensary was successful. I helped the dispensary reach sales beyond $2.6 million in six months and over $6 million in sales within one year. We were successful because we created a system, and we had a team of people that we trained to be successful. My contribution was enormous. I quickly saw that, what I could do for others within this industry on a larger scale, I could do for myself.

My statement was created from a place of divine inspiration birthed from frustration, peace, and then stillness. I hadn't felt acknowledged or appreciated for my work. I was determined to bring success to the dispensary, and I was open to receive what the universe had for me beyond this moment. If you don't feel appreciated after you've made people millions, you know it's time to branch out. I focused on love while working in the dispensaries, and the patients always made my work worthwhile. Shortly after I wrote my initial statement, I experienced lots of growth and rapid expansion. I narrowed my focus to the CBD industry, and my cannabis entrepreneur journey continues to grow, unfold, and expand in exciting ways.

Earl Nightingale is quoted to have said, most people don't succeed because they don't know what they want. Some know *what* they want and do not know *why* they want it. You must know both elements if you want to lead your industry. You don't have to know the exact path that you will take. You have to know what you came here to do, what gifts you plan to contribute, how much money you want to make doing it, and whom you wish to serve with your product or service. You have to have passion when you create your statement; passion gives fuel to your *why*. If you want to be a leader within your industry, setting goals fueled by passion is a recipe for success. Leaders with a burning passion can gain momentum and support from others. They stand out amongst their competitors because they are driven by more. You can market your passion and share your enthusiasm with your customers.

I've seen this play out in my role as a cannabis entrepreneur. Identifying my *why* is the reason that within five months of launching my CBD company, I had several offers from investors to buy my company. I envisioned what I wanted in advance and why I wanted it—knowing *what* and *why* forms the pathway to victory. That doesn't mean everything works out exactly as you visualized yet having a plan will help you get closer to your target.

My initial statement blossomed into: teach three million women who are driven to change the world in a loving way how to create quality CBD products that maintain the healing integrity of the sacred plant. In other words, to help people create CBD products that they can be proud to give to their families and share with the world. The statement declares my desire to share with 3 million women my passion for the plant and how it changed and transformed my life for the better, mentally, physically, and spiritually. This statement manifests today as my Consulting/Courses, CBD products, and Masterminds/Goddess retreats. Daily visualization helped me manifest my reality faster by keeping my reason for accomplishing my goals in the forefront of my mind. I started to notice business success when I started visualizing all the people that I wanted to help. I began to feel what it felt like to help so many people. The more I kept my *why* in my foresight, the stronger my will became to carry out my goals.

Identify Your Target

Once you've determined *what* you've come here to do and *why* you've come here to it, it's time to identify *whom* you want to serve. Narrowing your target audience will help you achieve success. Your target audience is a specific group of people who would be interested in your products or services. These people share the same characteristics, behaviors, and interests. Naming your target audience allows you to paint a picture of your ideal customer. Geographic, demographic, and psychographic are the three main ways you can find your target market. Businesses typically use demographic information to define their target audience. Examples of standard demographic information include gender, age, location, profession, income, education levels, and marital status.

What does the person look like that you want to serve? Where do they live? What do they like? Identifying your target audience helps you strategically spend your marketing and advertising dollars. You save money and time because you have narrowed your focus to a select group of individuals who are more likely to buy your product. You are not playing a guessing game. And you are not throwing your money at every marketing idea because you know which mediums work best for communicating with your people. You've done your homework. You also get to know your audience by studying what they like and what they don't like. You know what types of websites they visit and how they get their information. Because you know your target, you know exactly where to market and advertise.

When you know whom you want to reach and you speak directly to your audience, you are likely to reach the ears you want. Identifying your target audience helps you to talk in your customers' language and grab their attention with your product. You may decide to target mothers ages 25-45, creating a product catering to them, such as a CBD spa box kit. The kit contains a CBD infused peppermint foot scrub, herbal CBD tea, and coconut CBD bath bombs, for example. You cut through the crowd by getting your offer in front of the eyes of your target group. You can't be everything to everyone, but you can provide exactly what someone desires. Getting your offer in front of potential customers is a step closer to finding their needs, meeting them, and closing the sale. Not knowing whom you are marketing your offer to is like going on a blind date with no background check. You don't know to whom you are talking. You could be going out with anyone! When you target your audience, you know exactly to whom you are talking. Finding your target is a customer vetting process. Narrowing your focus increases the probability of hitting your target.

Knowing your target audience helps you to understand the problems your target audience faces. It helps you to generate solutions for that audience. When you have identified whom you want to serve, you speak to them and directly ask them what they want. You build a relationship with the people who are interested in your products. Customers that feel heard will start trusting you with their money. Speaking to your target audience helps you to develop better products and services using audience feedback. You have found their wants, needs, and preferences. Your target audience will tell you what works for them. They will tell you what they like, don't like and why they don't like it. That's the type of information you need to create products that your customers will purchase and enjoy. One of the dispensaries where I worked was attached to a pain management clinic. Being so close to the clinic, our advertising efforts, quality of products, and branding, brought in a tremendous amount of baby boomer patients. Our patients would give us feedback regularly and share what worked for them and what did not. Their feedback was immensely helpful. We couldn't afford to put anything less than the best on the shelves. We valued our patients' experiences with the products we sold, and that's why the dispensary reached millions of dollars in sales quickly.

Smart business owners listen to their audience. Your customers can help you grow because they can give you ideas. They tell you what they want to buy. I can remember when I moved to the Carlsbad area. I found a cute crystal store nearby and gave the store managers ideas of what they could add to the store to make it even better. I recommended adding CBD, oracle cards, and soothing light music to add to the store's ambiance. Within a few months of making the recommendation, I returned to the store only to find that they had added all of my suggestions. I watched their store transform before my eyes. I watched the store traffic increase because they increased their offers (with the right products). The owners receive my customer loyalty because they listen to their customers. I love supporting their business. Your customer feedback can help you discover where to put your focus, where you need to improve, what's working, and so on. When you put the information, you receive from your demographic to skillful use to build your company, you win!

Pinpointing whom you want to influence and solidifying your brand personality will help you gain brand recognition and loyalty. A brand is a unique design, sign, symbol, words, or a combination of these, employed in creating an image that identifies a product and differentiates the product from its competitors. Over time, this image becomes associated with a level of credibility, quality, and satisfaction in the consumer's mind. Thus, brands help consumers in a crowded and complex marketplace by standing for certain benefits and value. The legal name for a brand is called a *trademark*. When the imagery names or represents a firm, it is called a *brand name*—knowing your brand personality will teach you how to talk to your potential customer. It helps to develop the psychological mood that you want to create. Knowing your brand puts you in the heads of your customers. You get to decide what type of feeling you want your tribe to have.

The goal of brand personalities is to anchor your brand against something iconic, concepts already embedded within the human conscious and subconscious. I discuss brand archetypes in detail in Key 3 within this book. In the minds of both the brand owner and the public, aligning with a brand image makes the brand more natural to find. It also helps the brand personality stand out. You get to decide what brand personality works best for your company. I teach my clients how to show their brand personality clearly.

Your brand personality will help you select the *right* voice to use when reaching out to your target. Your brand personality will guide you on which colors and tones to use throughout your business branding. Part of setting up your business is knowing what your business brand looks like. There are 12 common brand personality types. Identifying your brand personality can help you refine (*precisely*) what you are selling. Beyond products and services, you are selling your customers a lifestyle. For example, Harley Davidson would fit into the rebel brand personality type. Beyond selling cool Harley bikes and Harley gear, Harley sells the image that everyone can be a badass on the weekend. With a Harley, no matter what you do during the week, how many kids you have at home, or how many churches you pastor, you are a weekend badass. Harley Davidson is an excellent example of how uniting a community under an image makes customers feel like they belong to something greater. They become empowered consumers. Harley's rebellious image creates unity among their followers and fans. When your branding speaks the same brand message consistently in all marketing platforms, you connect to your customers (beyond just making another sale). You are on your way to creating an iconic sellable brand.

Knowing your target helps you create allies that will spread your brand message. And consistent quality leads to more sales. When you are reliable, you earn repeat customers. You want to build a brand that's synonymous with quality. People support quality brands. Your brand becomes part of their lifestyle. People like to share things that add value to their lives. And new customers want to buy products from companies their friends recommend. Customers will support your business if you continue to give them a reason to support it.

Customers who like your products, resonate with your message, and feel like they are part of your community will want to spread your message. They will want to proclaim from the mountain tops how awesome you are. They will want to share the news with everyone they know. These customers become more than customers; some become friends. They become supporters. Some customers love what you do so much; they offer to be your affiliate. Affiliates are people who sell your product or service for a percentage of the sale. Affiliates are people who ideally love you and what you offer. They also see an opportunity to get paid for doing what they enjoy doing—sharing information. To use vetted affiliates to sell your products, create an affiliate sign-up link on your website.

Adding an affiliate program to your business is an excellent option for a start-up because it's performance-based and can help spread your brand message. Some customers who become affiliates already have lists of the kinds of people that want your products. The more they share about you with others, the warmer the leads you generate. Warm leads from affiliates have higher conversion rates compared to cold leads. Adding an affiliate program gives customers who want to support your company an opportunity to make money and promote your company. By creating an opportunity for your customers, you create a solution where everyone benefits. You make your business stand out by rallying support. You turn clients into fans by giving them a reason to care.

Paying people gives them a reason to care because you are allowing them to transform their finances. If your brand gives back, you have a bonus, because you think of others beyond yourself. Who does your brand benefit beyond your company? Some customers will choose you over the competition because you give back. They want to feel like they are part of something greater without leaving their living rooms. It's up to you and your marketing team to make your customers feel like they are part of the vision.

You must know the vision and not be afraid to dream a fucking big dream. This is my advice for any entrepreneur. Yet, it is especially my advice for people who have felt held back because of skin color and gender. When you create a brand that captivates, you gain the attention of your customers repeatedly. You delight your customers when you dare to dream big.

Dream a Big Dream

First, African American woman, you need to know that you can dream big just like everyone else. You have the freedom to dream big. Despite the odds, enormous success is attainable for those bold enough to pursue it. It's time for you to stop playing small. It's time to expect fucking more! What does it mean to expect fucking more? It means daring to dream big, having the audacity to be more than average, stepping outside of the box and your comfort zone and visualizing the life that you want, even if it seems impossible to attain. If you dream it, you can achieve it, as the saying goes. The more impossible the idea appears, the better because you're likely to hit a target.

You have to be able to visualize the outcome. You want to have a clear picture of where you are going and visualize where you want to be. The

74

outcome is what success looks like to you. Ask yourself what kind of car you would drive in five years. What kind of house are you living in, or do you have an apartment? What country are you living in? Do you have children? Are you married? The key is to be as specific as possible. The clearer that you see yourself in the future, the better because that will steer you in the right direction on what type of business to create.

In 2012, I asked African American women business owners to describe the process of how they decided to start their own business. What led them to choose this type of business? I wanted to explore the decision-making processes of the entrepreneurs who started their companies and probe their motivation for starting such companies. The answers to this question and others gave me insight into the critical factors for entrepreneurs in the brainstorming and developmental stages of their companies. Research by Cummings (1999) suggests that African American entrepreneurs are more attracted to specific entrepreneurial ventures. Such as service industries, because of the ease of starting these businesses, and the limited capital required. Four out of five respondents I interviewed operated service industry companies[60].

Service industries are defined as industries that produce mostly intangible value, such as customer service, management advice, knowledge, design, data, and experiences. Examples of service industry businesses are accounting, personal fitness trainers, and make-up artists. A service business is a business in which you and your employees work primarily providing services. A *non-service* business is one in which your business sells mostly tangible products, CBD face wash, for example. There is a lot of business opportunity within the service industries. There is also lots of competition because of the low barrier to entry. You can create your blue ocean and stand out by creating a plan[64]. You can expand beyond the service industry and grow your business by adding products, for example. But before you expand, you must have a strategy. Establish a business plan and consider how to grow beyond your initial service offerings. Think expansion when you think entrepreneur, think beyond survival. Create a plan, start your business with development in mind, plan to grow into your business, do more, and reach more.

Think of ways you can grow and advance. Establish the purpose of your business first. Your purpose statement is found by asking yourself: What is the change you want to bring about in the world? Sit down with yourself, goddess. What is the reason your organization exists? What is the idea that launched your company? Then you must determine how you plan on accomplishing your purpose. What will be your way? How will you go about achieving your goals?

Your approach is your organization's strategy; it is the way you move and get things done. What is your blueprint? How will you get from here to there? How do you go about getting things done? Your way helps you move forward with your plan. You must include and track your success milestones to ensure your business is moving forward and progressing. You must keep track of your business and determine if it's meeting the standards that you have set up within your company. You do this by having a check and balancing system in place. You must have a system in place that evaluates the execution of your strategic plan. This system may also check if there is room for improvement. You must set up a standard for success before you launch your company. And if you want more success, then you can always improve your standard and grow.

Your *how* is inspired by your organizational culture and values. Your organizational culture is also called corporate culture. It can affect four areas:

- the ways the organization conducts its business, treats its employees, customers, and the wider community,
- the extent to which freedom is allowed in decision making, developing new ideas, and personal expression,
- how power and information flow through its hierarchy, and
- how committed employees are towards collective objectives.

As a business owner, you also need to know your impact. Your impact is the way you want to affect the lives of others. What do you want the outcome to look like? Your impact is how your world would look if you carry out your purpose. Your impact is also your payoff (what success looks like for you, how much money you want to make, how many people you want to help). Brainstorming your purpose, way, and the purpose's impact can help you gain clarity and create your entrepreneurial vision. All these pieces can come together to form an amazing idea. You need to know that you can do more than own a business. You can effect change. Yes, as an African American woman. You can make a difference. Key phrases such as "wanting to be my own boss, become independent and doing what I wanted to do," formed part of the thought process that motivated study participants to become entrepreneurs.

The participants shared,

> I was working in medical software for a vendor, and I knew I wanted a certain lifestyle several years after I started working for that vendor. I knew I wanted to be independent, so I didn't want to work for anyone else; at least that was a starting point for me. (R01)

> I wanted to do things that I liked to do. The first business I had on my own was selling Tupperware. I was about 22 years old when I started that. It felt good to make my own money, plan my own hours, and do what I wanted to do. (R05)

The lack of real job security, displeasure with the corporate world, lack of promotions within the corporate world, and the realization of their skills were also reasons why the respondents became entrepreneurs. One out of the five asserted that a company lay-off inspired entrepreneurialism. At the same time, four out of the five saw entrepreneurialism as a way to use their skills to create the lifestyle they desired.

> I was one of the people who were laid off. I had always worked a job, so the layoff was a shocker. My only saving grace was my ability to do taxes, so the company kept me on for a couple of more weeks to help with its payroll and other tax functions. The company needed me because I had the skill to do taxes; having this skill was an eye-opener for me. I got a second job based on my skill to do taxes. While working on the second job, I thought

about the fact that I was previously laid off from my other job. It always played in my head that people who owned the business were not laid off; I wanted to be in that place. It was through the layoff experience that I figured I needed to become an entrepreneur; I needed to work for my own company. (R02)

I worked in corporate for a few years, and I did not enjoy working in the corporate world, so I thought that being my own boss would be the way to go. (R03)

I got tired of working hard for someone else. I got tired of someone else using my customer service skills while I improved their business. I got tired of not being promoted, with the ability to get fired at any time. (R04)

Being your own boss is just the beginning. When I entered the cannabis industry, I set a vision to become the number one woman in the cannabis trade. In 2018, my partner and I created the first CBD consulting company in the World. When I wrote my vision, however, I didn't have a CBD company or knowledge that I was going to create one. If you recall from my story earlier, I was working for someone else during the time I wrote my cannabis industry vision. My goal was lofty, to say the least, yet it's better to have a high goal because you create momentum to achieve something great. Even if you don't hit your mark, you will still achieve greatness. Dreaming big means creating an idea that scares you because it seems impossible— like becoming the number one woman in the cannabis space. Because I set my goals high, I carved out a niche for myself. I became Number One within that niche. Initially, it may not be clear exactly how you will achieve the vision that you set for yourself. Please know that anything is possible. And be open to all of the wonderful possibilities.

You may brainstorm the different things that you can do to achieve your goals and then start the process of eliminating some of those things. One goal will lead to accomplishment; one failure will lead to another opportunity. There is no right or wrong move. All of these "things" that happen to you on your entrepreneur path will lead to exactly where you need to be because you set your intention. You dared to dream big. Persistence is the key. Before I became a CBD consultant, I created a successful CBD brand. I helped to open several dispensaries and delivery services. I had no intention of becoming a CBD consultant. Still, through my experience and persistence within the cannabis space, that is where the universe led me.

The best part about being an entrepreneur is the ability to create meaningful business ventures that incorporate my values. As an entrepreneur, you get to create something unique to you. You get to become a master creator and do something with meaning, on a grand scale. You can expand beyond doing what people expect you to do; you can push beyond what others consider the norm and build an empire with generational wealth! You can do more than start a non-profit or small-scale business. That is fine, too, if that's what your heart desires.

Another cool thing about being an entrepreneur is the ability to get paid to do what your heart loves. Dreaming big means daring to create a business you enjoy, that makes an impact, and stretches you. An entrepreneur that dreams big will think beyond creating a product line. They will build a storefront to help them sell their product line and expand their brand exposure. The impact you make with your business can become global. It's time for African American women to stop playing small. It's time to eliminate the word *can't* and replace it with *can*. Dreaming big and expecting more, is not off-limits to us!

Develop Your Success Routine

Successful people are people who plan to be successful. Successful business owners have several habits in common. One way to be effective and achieve your goals quicker is to create a solid routine. Routines help you create the blueprint for achievement. It's a systematic process that you complete consistently, preferably using a checklist. Another habit is writing things down. Put those both together (routine + writing things down), and you have a magical formula for getting things done. Routines help you to develop a pattern. You can choose the pattern you want to program within your life. One way to create a routine is to repeat a task for 21 days, for example, if one of your goals is to get up early, start getting up at your desired time for 21 days. After 21 days, you create a pattern within your mind, thus creating a habit. You want to make it a habit to set up a solid routine. You can start today if you have not already.

Reasons to Create Business Routines

Routines help you to improve your business's **Organization**. Established routines hold you accountable for your time because you become aware of what you are doing and when. Let your routine be thoughtful and strategic, in that it becomes purposeful. Establishing a routine can help you improve the organization of your day-to-day schedule, which will help you strategically achieve your goals. When you become a master of your time, you will have all the time in the world to get things done. Part of that proficiency is knowing and acting like your time is valuable. When you create a routine, you make better use of your time, which leads to the next benefit of establishing a routine.

Routines help you improve your **Task Management** by helping you get things done. This outcome may seem obvious; however, you'd be surprised how many people don't know how an effective routine can improve task management. They say the devil is in the details, and this is certainly true for business owners who strive to achieve more. Usually, when you decide you want more out of life, you are presented with opportunities-that *you create* for yourself-so that you can achieve more.

When you want more, then more is required of you. For example, you have an e-commerce CBD company that's selling body oils that are doing fantastic. Within the first year of launching your company, you managed to net $200K. (This is not impossible, yet no easy feat, since most businesses do not net $200K within their first year of sales). Nevertheless, in Year One of launching your CBD body oil company, you netted $200K. As a result, you feel that you have enough capital to expand your brand into retail. Taking a product from e-commerce sales and expanding into retail takes tremendous planning and organization. This planning requirement is genuine whether you wholesale your products to other stores or create your own retail space as an extension of your brand. A business goal like this is going to require some strategic planning. A plan becomes strategic when it meets five requirements. One, the plan is organized. Two, the plan outlines what needs to be done. Three, the plan identifies who's doing what. Four, the plan specifies what's required to get the task done, along with the financial cost, if any. Five, the plan sets the deadlines for getting the tasks done. If you have big goals like branching from e-commerce to a brick and mortar, then you may have to organize several strategic plans with sizable tasks to accomplish your retail goal.

Routines turn **Big Ideas into Daily Doable Pieces.** Big ideas can sometimes be intimidating or impossible to accomplish. You learn how to prioritize. Every day you review what you must get done that day. Even if you don't complete all of your tasks for that day, you are golden. You add those items to your task list for the following day and make a goal to complete those tasks. The secret to completing your list is to create a list of things you know you will do. You have to be honest with yourself. If you start with a list of 30 daily tasks, for example, and you find you are not completing them regularly, then perhaps you need to do fewer tasks. Perhaps instead of having a list of 30 tasks, you create a list with 6 to 10 higher priority tasks. This way, you take the quality over quantity task completion approach and cross high priority items off your list. While doing your routine and creating your tasks, you may also discover that you have time to complete more tasks. You may find that it makes sense for you to complete 15 tasks in a day.

Tasks keep you moving. Establishing routines allow you to eat the figurative elephant, one spoonful at a time. Perhaps the task itself is challenging, and therefore, you procrastinate over getting it done. Routines help you overcome procrastination by getting you in the habit of crossing things off a list. I recommend making a daily task checklist as a part of your routine. Every day you want to make a list of 6 to 10 tasks to accomplish. I like to add some personal tasks within my list because managing my personal life is just as important as managing my business life. If your personal life is unorganized, that may lead to stress and loss of focus on your business. Routines keep you on track because every day, you see what you need to do and what you have already done. You get the sense that you are moving forward because you are! You are moving forward towards achieving your objectives. Routines help you to reach your goals and not just fantasize about what you want to do. Completion of daily tasks moves you closer to your destiny.

Routines encourage **Accountability and Consistency**. Establishing routines will show where there is room for improvement and chart your progress as a developing business owner. Routines are things you do daily. Over time, *doing* your routine enables you to gauge your business progress. Sometimes when I feel stuck within my business and not making progress or reaching my business goals, I review my routine. I take a good look and analyze what I've been doing with my time. Routines allow you to correct or change a course of action. Routines keep you responsible and help you troubleshoot. I feel more in control when I have a routine because I have a plan. I have a course of action for the day that I can tweak at any time, if necessary. Routines supply a map that keeps you on track.

Developing a Routine for Success

There are many ways to develop your success routine. The first tip is to **Listen to the Eternal Rhythm of Your Body and Start Your Workday from There.** Create your routine from your natural body's rhythm. Grow where you are planted. Don't beat yourself up if you find you are not a morning person, and you are not interested in getting up at 5 am. Your body knows what feels right to it, and when it is rested, it performs better. Your mind knows when it wants to work. It has been said that successful people wake-up in the wee hours of the morning, that's only partly true.

Waking up early in the morning is not a sole indicator of success. Although the early bird *can* catch the worm, there is no guarantee that just because you are awake that you are productive. Success is demonstrated by productivity. What do you *do* when you do get up? Are you crossing things off your business checklist? Are you closer to where you want to be with your business?

The key to success is going with the flow and knowing there is a time for everything. There is a time to be willing to work all hours, including early and late. If you didn't know, business owners work all sorts of crazy-ass hours. This condition is especially true as you build your business and learn to work smarter. The good news is that you are putting your time and energy into yourself when you work on your business. It is not unusual for business owners to be overwhelmed with work within the first few formative years if the business owner survives that long, or until they build a team around them.

When I started my first CBD brand with my partner, I had no idea about all of the work ahead of us, and we were no strangers to working our asses off within this industry! I felt like I was literally working around the clock, and I am sure my partner felt like he was working double-time—because he was! We had to rely mostly on ourselves. Which was stressful, I worked my body to the max. I never felt like I was doing enough even though we were successful, on track with our plan, and doing all that we could do.

I pushed my body and mind to the limit until one day, I experienced tremendous back pain that led me to tears, healing, and ultimately, to this epiphany. Listen to your body. Business owners typically work long hours indeed; however, you must learn balance. You must listen to your body and follow what it's telling you to do at that moment. Wisdom is essential, along with self-discipline. You also have to be self-controlled enough to know when to give yourself a break. And when to work like an animal. If you do overdo it, listening to your body can get you back on track.

The appropriate rhythm for your body may be determined by the type of business you have or want. For example, if you sell a service that requires you to exchange your time for money, you restrict your freedom a bit because you will have to be present to get paid. Yet, if you sell a product online, you may have more flexibility with your schedule and not have-to-have direct contact with your customers. Productivity is the name of the game. You can be productive and get up after 5 am. Find your sweet spot.

The second tip to improving your success routine is to **Plan Your Checklist the Night Before.** Your checklist is what you plan to do tomorrow. Some successful entrepreneurs have found that making decisions in the morning is a mental challenge. We all have been there. It can be a challenge to muster the willpower. I like to call it the Blank Paper Syndrome. I discovered that once you know what you have to do, and you have written it down, you have a clearer mind. You have peace of mind because you know what you must do. It's easier to brainstorm the tasks you have to complete when you are not under pressure to complete the *actual* task.

I like to call developing my plan, *freethinking* because you are brainstorming and listing what has to be done the next day. The freedom comes from not being obligated to complete tasks at that very moment. You can relax while you write. When you are relaxed, it's easier to think about what you have to do. Planning your routine the night before is a powerful key because it puts you ahead of the challenge of "Starting." Doing things early, while you are relaxed, saves you the stress of figuring out what you have to do and doing it too. Writing things down the night before breaks up your tasks and helps you to manage your time better. Doing small favors for yourself in advance is setting yourself up for success. You are more inclined to get going and accomplish things if you know what to do first. And your thinking will be reserved for the task at hand; you won't waste your time thinking about what you have to do. If you take care of your hardest challenge, which often is starting, you can be ahead of the curve. This is a wonderful secret!

I enjoy writing my checklist at night. Because, the nighttime is when I am fully awake and ready to create. It makes writing a checklist easy, even fun. My work schedule varies. I adjust my schedule based on whether or not I have special projects. Consequently, I may work additional late hour shifts when I am writing and creating material to sell online. For example, right now, as I am typing this book, it's 1:13 am. It is not unheard of for me to go to bed at 3:30 am, and that's an early night. I've always been a night owl. I learned how to use my love for the night to benefit my business. I made my time useful. When I write my checklist the night before, it makes me feel like I am my own executive assistant, which is a job I've done for others, as an employee. I am better prepared for tomorrow. The key to success is to be prepared in advance. You want to see things coming beforehand and plan your move.

The third and final tip is to **Create an (Enjoyable) Morning Routine.** It's not enough to create a routine; I encourage you to establish a routine that you *enjoy* doing. Because if you don't enjoy the routine that you set for yourself, you are not likely to continue with the routine. This will hinder your progress. Keep your routine fresh and fun. You may want to add elements to your routine that improve your health: daily exercise, for example. Research suggests that exercising a few minutes every day can improve your mental health and increase your energy. Also, water is necessary as you release sweat when you exercise. Exercising gets the heart rate-up, relieves stress, and produces feel-good hormones.

There is a framework that successful business owners follow, and that's doing what works and what brings you results. Your routine may not look exactly like the next business owner's routine, although there may be similarities. You have to create something that works for you. It does not have to be precisely like my routine for you to be successful. There's plenty of wiggle room to be creative. You will tweak your routine because life will happen, just because you are a business owner does not mean that life stops. I like to add my life tasks to my routines to ensure that I am taking care of my home and business.

My morning routine helps to focus my mind. The contents of the morning routine are essential for consistency; a healthy routine sets the tone for the entire day. A daily routine helps to anchor and prepare you for what's next. It helps you to **Take charge and take action.** After you have set the tone for your day, it is time to take action. Pull out the task list that you created the night before and get busy.

My Morning Routine

Here is the gist of my morning routine, which certainly varies. The first thing I do is **Shower and take care of all hygiene.** This task makes me feel good. If you don't feel well, it's going to be challenging to work well. Taking care of my body is just as important as taking care of my business. I like to turn my shower and cleansing routine into a ritual by lighting sage, using natural soaps and attraction oils, and playing motivational music. I like to take my time and appreciate the sun. After I have completed my cleansing routine, and I've gotten dressed, I reach for my coffee and water. I am a **Coffee and water girl in the morning**. I am not a huge breakfast person; it takes a while for my appetite to kick in. An apple, coffee, and water is the perfect way for me to start my day. I like to ease into my morning. I love walking in the garden and enjoying my coffee slowly.

I do not start my day without meditation. And I love meditating with cannabis, particularly, sativas in the morning to enhance inspiration and creativity. Cannabis is legal in California, and that's another reason I love living here. I am certainly a fan of waking and baking in the morning, which means to enjoy cannabis when you arise. I like to enjoy my cannabis with coffee. What's not to love about this combination? There is a back road near my house that leads to an open field where I love to walk in the morning. When I get there, I meditate. Meditation is a huge part of my daily routine.

Meditation transforms my attitude and adds a layer of peace to my day. It has helped me tremendously with stress management. In addition to meditating, I love to play with my dog and catch up with my family. Listening to **Positive audiobooks in the morning** also helps to get me going mentally and inspires me. I love starting my day with Eckhart Tolle to help me stay within the present moment. Journaling in the morning is another part of my routine that helps me remain focused and clears my thoughts. Finally, after completing all of these things, I **Pull out my task list** from the night before and start working.

What I love the most about my routine is that it is stress-free. I remember when I worked for someone else, and I had to fight traffic to get to work at 6:45 am, sometimes 5:45 am! Do you know what time you have to get up to get to work by 5:45 am? Especially when it's snowing in Wisconsin? Early. You have to get up incredibly early. I've had to get up early all of my life for academic, professional, and recreational reasons. Yet, I've always been a night person. For years, as an entrepreneur, I struggled, because I thought that I had to do things the way that the *experts* suggested. Overworking myself led to back pain. I realized I had to create a routine that worked for me. I don't like working right away in the morning. I feel like my mind isn't ready. I prefer to meditate before I start my tasks because I want my mind to be in alignment with my heart when I do business throughout the day.

The right routine can make or break your business. Not creating a routine puts your business at risk of failure. Routines help you plan, stay focused, and remain active within your company. Routines create the rhythm that sets the tone for the day. Establishing a routine keeps you accountable. In 2018, I added a nightly routine to my daily routine. I did this so that I could finish my writing projects. By sticking to my routine, I was able to create and publish a CBD Success course, with over 300 slides, 30 handouts, and several videos within a few short months. If it were not for my nightly routine, which consists of me writing in intervals and taking breaks in-between, I would not stay committed to my writing projects.

Routines are especially important for getting past procrastination. Creating a routine kept me from quitting when I wanted to give up. If it weren't for being powered by routine, I would've listened to all my excuses when running a business became challenging. I wouldn't have had the stamina to continue as an entrepreneur had I not seen my work. A routine lays out your accomplished goals. By keeping track of what I do, I chart my progress. If I could not see where I've been, I would not remember how far I've come. I would've given up a long time ago. But when I look back over the years of project notebooks, and I look at where I am now, I can see that routines have helped me accomplish many of my personal and business goals—thereby giving me optimal success.

Key 3: Business Development

What is business development? Business development is the process of building your business. It's something that all entrepreneurs signup for the moment they choose to become a business owner. Business development is necessary if you want to start and grow your company. You should have a plan for company growth before starting your company. You should plan to grow. You should create a strategic plan and project where you see your company being from the beginning to its' end. You want to have a plan to leave within your blueprint too. For example, you may decide early on in your business model that you are creating your business to sell. Or you may want to create a franchise or multilevel company. The point is, you must develop your business and create the proper strategy to help you reach your business goals.

Business development happens in stages. Entrepreneurs tend to develop their business in stages influenced by the culture. The path of business development for entrepreneurs is as follows: **Idea:** it all starts with your divine spark, the moment you decide to become an entrepreneur. **Concept**: once you know you want to be an entrepreneur you start putting your ideas together. **Building**: at this stage, the entrepreneur is often gathering her resources to develop her business, to make her concepts concrete. **Growing:** At this stage, ideally, you've proven your business concept, with consistent customer service and increased sales. It is often at this stage that entrepreneurs look to capitalize on a good thing and grow their business through expansion and/or creating additional business offerings. The last stage for a business owner is **Exiting**. An exit is when an entrepreneur creates a departure plan. Those people that develop businesses should also be thinking about their next move. What will happen to your business when you are no longer working there, and how could you be affected?

One of my favorite exit strategies is selling my stake of the company to an investor or finding an acquirer to buy my company within a three- to five-year timeframe, from company launch.[56]

Develop Your Brand

Before you can set up your business, I recommend you learn and develop your brand. I recommend developing your brand before you create your company. Brands encourage customer devotion. Your brand is what sets you apart from your competitors. It makes you recognizable, and it can increase your business value by helping you gain competitive leverage. Investors love to invest in branded companies. Branding gives you a cohesive professional look, which can attract customers. Customers love to buy from brands that feel familiar. Branding creates trust in the marketplace. People are more likely to do business with brands they can trust.

Successful companies create strong brands that become household names. Branding also improves employee pride and satisfaction because it creates a sense of belonging, purpose, and helps to boost morale. Employees feel like they belong to something greater than selling products. Your brand is your story. Employees resonate with a story that they can believe and share with customers. Brands stand by an established set of beliefs and values. Branding helps you target your advertising, saving you money. Business owners can use branding to spread their brand message with promotional items.

Branding is an essential first step in the entrepreneurial process and business development. It's a foundational step, in that it lays the groundwork for how you represent your company. It showcases to your audience what matters to you while suggesting what should matter to your audience. Establishing your brand is a critical step because your brand sets the tone for your business. Successful business owners brand their companies within a brand archetype.

Knowing your business archetype gives your brand a framework to work in because each archetype is unique. Archetypes are a concept originally conceived by famed Swiss psychologist, Carl Jung. Archetypes are instinctive tendencies that shape human behavior. In marketing, a brand archetype is a genre you give to your brand based upon symbolism. The goal of brand archetypes is to anchor your brand against something iconic and concepts already embedded within the human conscious and subconscious. In the minds of both the brand owner and the public, aligning with a brand, archetype makes the brand easier to identify. It also helps the brand stand out. Your brand archetype is the personality of your brand. Establishing your brand archetype can help you, and your customers better understand your business. Sticking within a brand archetype can help you create brand recognition and brand cohesion. As a business owner, you want to create a brand identity to strengthen your brand. When you have a brand identity, you can create an emotional connection with buyers and tell your story. This is an essential piece of business development because if you can't reach and talk to your customers, you can't help them.

Creating an emotional connection with your customers can help you create the right products for your target audience. Telling your company's story will resonate with your chosen audience. Your brand identity will determine the flow of your brand. Your brand archetype helps you select the colors to use for marketing and how to speak directly to your customers. The brand archetype enables you to select imagery based on how you want your audience to feel and more. When you choose an archetype, you select it based on how you want your customers to feel when they experience your brand. Successful business owner's brands often fit into one of 12 universal brand archetypes: the nurturer, the ruler, the hero, the magician, the rebel, the seeker, the sage, the innocent, the orphan, the jester, the enchantress, and the creator.

The 12 Brand Archetypes

The nurturer. The nurturer is the mother archetype. The mother archetype always wants to take care of others; this is why this archetype is also known as the *caretaker* archetype. The mother archetype is one that gives a damn. They are the saints of the 12 universal archetypes. Because they care. They make sure they offer quality goods and services. Nurturers relate to their customers because they are close to their customers' needs. They know what their customers want because the nurturer listens, and they do their homework. You cannot be a nurturer without knowing what people need. They want to meet the needs of their customers through their products, services and helping humanity.

Nurturers are selfless brands that give back. They may have charitable causes they give back to; they may also offer extra savings to their customers. This type of business passes their business savings right along to the customer. The nurturer archetype is customer service and customer satisfaction driven. Nurturer businesses have a theme of helping their customers as their core model. This brand is very compassionate and willing to go the extra mile for their customers. If this brand was a person and you needed a shirt, it would give you the shirt off its back.

Customers feel safe and secure with nurturing brands; they don't feel like the business is trying to take advantage of them because nurturer brands are not self-motivated. Customers feel supported, important, and valued. The nurturer brand voice is thoughtful and considerate. Dove and Johnson & Johnson are examples of nurturer brands. Nurturer brands want their customers to feel supported.

The ruler. The ruler archetype is the power brand, the "one who is in control." The ruler is often a high-end brand. They are the leaders of the 12 universal archetypes. Rulers are dominant, accountable, reliable, and responsible. The ruler governs with high standards. This kind of brand is considered a leader within their industry. Rulers create a feeling of prosperity, security, and stability for their consumers. This brand archetype cuts through the bullshit and chaos by maintaining order with policies and procedures.

The ruler archetype drives others to success and creates products and services that contribute and add value to others. Their offerings make their customers stand out within their community. Ruler brands often represent high-end goods and services by personifying wealth and power. Customers feel connected to wealth and success. Ruler brands want their customers to feel wealthy, powerful, and established. Rolex and Mercedes are examples of ruler brands; both of these companies exemplify a position of authority. Customers feel confident and exclusive when they purchase from these brands. The customers know they are buying into the best.

The hero. The hero archetype is the champion brand. They are the victorious ones within the 12 universal archetypes. This brand personality hits its target and achieves its goals. It's similar to the ruler brand because it's powerful and self-confident. The main difference is that the hero brand is less controlling and more courageous than the ruler brand. Heroes are winners. They aim to leave a winning legacy. This brand wants to make their mark on the world. They aim to inspire their customers to achieve more. The hero brand strives to improve the world and make it a better place. The hero brand type is competent; they know how to execute well on the goods and services they offer. Heroes are strong and confident. They pride themselves on good quality compared to their competitors. Customers feel secure with hero brands because of the consistent results that hero brands provide. They know that hero brands get things done. Hero customers feel ahead of the other customers. They can trust that the hero brand is going to deliver a quality product every time. Nike and the United States Marines are examples of hero brands. Customers feel inspired and motivated by hero brands.

The magician. The magician brand is the brand that makes dreams come true. They are the visionaries of the 12 universal archetype brands. This brand lives its vision. Magicians are inventive and charismatic leaders. They are mavericks that seek to understand how the universe works so that they can leverage their success and the success of others. They invent new ways of doing things that transform their clients' lives. Magician brands are always interested in creating original methods and discovering new solutions. Magicians are outside of the box and mainly concerned with creating magical experiences for their customers; they are also known as *healers*. The magician archetype dares their customers to dream big. In fact, they want to make their customers' wildest visions come true. Customers feel like they can do anything, and they dream big. Magicians create a world that's imagined first in the customer's mind and then made concrete in the world of form. They have wild imaginations. Magicians are uncontrollable. Customers feel privileged to bask in the glow of the magician brand. Their lives are transformed, and ultimately, customers glow like the brand they admire so much. MAC, Oprah, and Disney are examples of magician brands.

The rebel. The rebel brand is the brand that does what it wants, when it wants, and how it wants. It's the brand that's going to "go left" when everyone else is "going right." This brand trusts its gut. You have to have plenty of guts to be the rebel brand. Rebels establish their own rules because they find it hard to fit into the mold of other people's rules. They decide what works best for them, and they are adamant about being true to themselves. They pass this feeling on to their customers. The customer feels unique; they are proud to be outside of the status quo. They are happy to break barriers if that means listening to their own voice. The rebel goes with what feels right and authentic. The rebel is the cool kid at the playground. Instead of dimming its light and forcing its way into circles, the rebel makes you want to join their circle. Customers find that their voice echoes with the rebel brand. Virgin, Harley Davidson, and MTV are examples of rebel brands.

The seeker. The seeker brand is always looking for another way. They are on a mission to find and deliver the best. They seek constant improvement and evolution. There is always another way things can be done according to the seeker; they will find out what that way is. The seeker comes to destroy the old way of doing something. They constantly bring in new fresh ideas to help others. They are determined to explore many ways to solve one challenge. Customers feel lucky to purchase from a brand that is always exploring and generating products and services that are cutting edge. Seekers stay above the curve because they are always exploring new ways. Customers feel advanced. Starbucks, National Geographic, and Red Bull are examples of the seeker brand.

The sage. The sage brand is the one who knows. This brand is the wise brand of the 12 universal archetypes. This brand does its homework like the seeker, yet it also applies wisdom gained from experience. The sage is someone who can see problems before they arise and provide their customers with insider information. The sage is the brand that can see what's often not readily obvious to the public. Usually, the sage is first to know what's going on. They are the keeper of information. They are ahead because they are informed. Customers feel like they are in good hands. Customers feel educated and well informed. Google, NPR News, and *The Wall Street Journal* are examples of the sage brand.

The innocent. The innocent archetype is the optimist of the 12 universal brand archetypes. Like babies, they are pure and saint-like. They approach the world with a sense of wonder, amusement, and curiosity. The innocent brand feels wholesome. They communicate with their customers, reaching customers with their message of openness and transparency. This brand is lighthearted and youthful. They love to spread their message of love and charity for all humans. This archetype is kind and compassionate. Customers feel playful. Snuggle, McDonald's, and Coca-Cola are examples of the innocent brand.

The orphan. The orphan archetype is the average Joe of the 12 universal brand archetypes. They are the realist. Another name for the orphan is *the guy next door*. The orphan brand is down to earth and practical. They have virtues, and they accept everyone. An orphan is not a pretentious brand. They admire the ordinary man. An orphan brand is a brand that customers can see themselves in; it's a relatable archetype. The orphan values the individuality of each person; in fact, they respect that uniqueness. Orphan brands are people oriented. It's a brand for everyone. Their customers feel included; they feel like they belong. Ikea, eBay, and Trader Joes are examples of the orphan brand.

The jester. The jester is the jokester of the 12 universal brand archetypes. They like to spread enjoyment and keep things light. The jester brand doesn't take itself too seriously. The jester is at peace within the chaos of the world. They can lift any mood and bring fun to anything they do. Jesters use humor to illuminate the hypocrisy of the world. They level the playing field between the powerful and those who don't have power. The jester is high-spirited; they invite their customers to partake in a self-critical form of sarcasm. Customers feel tickled. Jesters put their customers at ease with their silliness. Skittles, Geico, and Budweiser are examples of the jester brand.

The enchantress. The enchantress is the goddess of the 12 universal brand archetypes. The goddess is dark, passionate, mysterious, and sexy. This is the enticer brand. This archetype pulls in customers by seducing them with stimulating offers. The enchantress appeals to the senses and loves advertising. This archetype brand keeps its customers anticipating what's next. The enchantress brands are experts at creating build-up and momentum with their target audiences. The customers feel pleasure when they experience the enchantress brand. Chanel, Victoria's Secrets, and Godiva are examples of the enchantress brand.

The creator. The creator brand is the inventor of the 12 universal brand archetypes. If it doesn't exist, it's because the creator hasn't made it yet. They love inventing. This brand is one that thrives from taking risks. They are willing to do whatever it takes if it means designing a product that provides solutions for their customers. The creator brand is extremely ambitious; they will find a unique way to get the job done! These are your nonconformists similar to the rebel brand, yet the creator archetype is more imagination driven. Customers feel comforted to connect with a brand that's true to itself. Apple, Lego, and Crayola are examples of the creator brand.

Develop Your Resources

Business development is vital at every stage. When you set up your business, you are creating a game plan, and you are formulating your company's image. You are creating a framework for how you want to be seen as a business entity. To be successful, you must start with a concept of who you are. This concept will develop for your company over time as you grow into what you wish to become, and as you allow yourself to expand into all that you can be. From the moment of business conception, you brainstorm all of these amazing ideas. Yet, you, like other entrepreneurs, may find you have limited resources to realize your dreams. Now what? Should you simply give up? Hell no. Sometimes you have to ask yourself, "What would Oprah do?" Oprah would make a way out of no way. And so can you! You have to think out of the box.

There are many ways to be creative and develop your business, even with limited resources. For example, you may not have the budget for office space, yet if you start an online business, you can work from anywhere and not require any office space. My business is remote. I can be anywhere and do what I do. I love the freedom that having a remote business gives me. I can live virtually anywhere in the world and not have to rely on finding new customers within that country to sustain my business. That is true freedom!

African American female business owners may not have all of the assets at their disposal. You may be starting your entrepreneurial journey with limited business managerial experience, financial resources, family support, or network connections. Nevertheless, you can still be successful if you are creative and resourceful. When you become desperate for success, you become resourceful. An African American woman's creativity is her ultimate asset. You have to dream big and also have realistic expectations at the same time. You have to know that when you open a business that not everyone in your life will support your entrepreneurial journey, and that's ok. You have to know that there were people who came before you, who looked like you, had less, and did more!

A successful business owner starts! They start. Right where they are with what they have. Start with the tools you have readily at your disposal. Start where you are. According to my doctoral research, African American women benefit from using outside employment as a platform to develop their own business. Working for someone else, especially working for a company that is similar to what you want to create, helps you to sharpen your skills as you transition into a business owner. My study of African American female business owners revealed that they researched their employers' business operations to gain field knowledge before they became independent business owners.

One respondent stated:

> Before I branched out, I worked for a larger franchise that provided tax services. I worked with them for a year during tax season, prior to going out on my own. My goal while I worked for the company was mentorship-driven; I wanted to understand how it operated. I watched what the people in the company did and how files were maintained. I worked there for the purposes of getting a grasp on how the tax industry worked. (R02)

I asked African American female business owners to describe the process of how they started their businesses. The data revealed that participants used their outside work experiences to develop their field and product knowledge. One respondent stated:

> I was working in medical software for a vendor, and I knew I wanted a certain lifestyle several years after I started working for that vendor. I knew I wanted to be independent. I chose to stay around four years to get all of the knowledge, training, and experience that I could because it was better to get it directly from the vendor. And then I chose to branch out from there...I said I'm going to get all the experience that I can until I feel comfortable enough to step out away from the vendor. So, from there, I went to a third-party consulting company. I was still working for somebody at that point, but I just kind of wanted to get that experience away from the vendor before I went independent on my own. (R01)

Working for someone while strategically making strides to work for yourself, is a viable strategy. One of the best books I ever read, *Caught Between a Dream and Job,* explores this strategy. The author talks about the bridge of wanting to become a business owner and working for someone else. There is a bridge that all would-be entrepreneurs must cross at some point if they hope to work for themselves. This bridge is scary because aspiring entrepreneurs often fear to let go of the familiar for the unfamiliar. They may not feel capable of supporting their lives financially, or they may not believe that they can be successful business owners. When you work for someone else, you have a significant opportunity to grow as an entrepreneur *before* you quit your 9 to 5 job. This opportunity is what African American women have to learn to use to their full advantage. Working for others can help you build your expertise. The professional world can prepare you for running your own company.

Working Like a CEO While You are an Employee

Act like a CEO while you're still an employee. Working like a CEO is going to put you in the right mindset, the mindset of a business owner, not a regular employee. A regular employee is typically not going to go the extra mile after they've completed their standard tasks. However, an employee that thinks like a successful CEO is going to complete their tasks, *and* they are going to see if anyone else needs help. An employee with a CEO mindset is going to do more than expected of them. When you adopt a CEO mindset in advance, you will improve your odds of business success. You grow in accountability when you lead as an employee. You benefit from acting like you are the CEO while you are yet an employee. Acting the part will, one, attract that vibration to you and, two, better mentally equip you when you become the CEO of your own company. This statement is not to say to literally take over someone else's company or assume that you are in charge. To clarify, I am suggesting that you strive to be a CEO in your head, even as you work for someone else.

When I worked in the Chief of Staff's office within the Federal government in Milwaukee, Wisconsin, I desperately wanted to break free. Still, I knew it was not time for me to leave because I wanted to develop my managerial skills. I was not in a management position, but I treated my job like I was the CEO. I managed myself, worked overtime, took on challenging projects, and became a master at completing tasks. When I attended meetings, (*in my mind*), I pretended that I was attending a business meeting for my company. I thought myself into the position that I wanted and knew I was capable of handling. It wasn't enough for me to remain as an Assistant to the Boss. I had a dream to become my own boss. I practiced being a boss while I was an assistant. I put my energy toward being the best assistant that I could be. My reviews were always fantastic. I reviewed myself before being reviewed by my manager. I kept track of myself. I remained accountable.

I advanced in both challenging and welcoming work environments. Every time I advanced and was promoted, I learned a new skill or sharpened an old skillset. My jobs became my business while I practiced being an entrepreneur and got paid to develop my skills. You become a successful business owner when you decide to be successful where you are. This guidance applies whether you are an employee who has just started your company, or a seasoned business owner seeking to learn a specific expertise. No matter your current position, you can learn to treat your role as if it was the most essential, critical position. Doing so is going to improve the quality of your job, and you will also attract a positive work experience while you grow as an entrepreneur. This path is what I experienced. If you are great at your job, you will get rewarded with more opportunities to grow. You will thank yourself later.

Doing more as an employee will keep you from settling for mediocracy, doing the status quo, what's required of you only. There is nothing wrong with average, yet, if you want to be successful, strive to be better than you were yesterday. Be a go-getter as an employee. Get in the rhythm of what you wish to become now. Regardless of where you are, you can immediately transform your job into your classroom. As you learn to overcome the odds within your work environment, know that to be a successful entrepreneur, you must know how to overcome the odds. Otherwise, business challenges may overtake you. Learn how to manage your stress levels while you are working for someone else. You will discover that it becomes easier for you to handle stressful situations when you are a business owner. When you overcome massive personal and professional odds, you can take this energy (of accomplishment) with you as a business owner. You have it in you to surpass average when you put in extra work and go the extra mile while you are an employee. A successful entrepreneur will shine as an employee first. A great work ethic will always pay off. When you develop your work ethic, you create exchangeable proficiencies that can cultivate your business and person.

Develop Transferable Skills

You may choose to branch out and become an entrepreneur within your current career path. You may decide to switch career paths altogether. Two of the five entrepreneurs that I interviewed had little to no understanding of their field of business before selecting it as their industry of choice. R01 reflected, "Actually, I knew nothing about med software consulting 10 years ago; I fell into it...when someone referred me to these companies online, and [I] applied for a position." R05 explained, "I don't have a background in journalism or anything, so this business came as an assignment from God." You may decide that you want to be an entrepreneur within an unfamiliar industry. If you take this route, you can still learn transferable skills that you can use within your business.

One of the advantages of outside employment is all the on-the-job training that you get for free. I worked as a professional within the various career paths and developed many efficiencies and personal skills. Transferable skills are those proficiencies that you learn or sharpen over a lifetime of experiences, both work-related and not work-related. I worked and morphed into a full-time entrepreneur. There is no right or wrong way. You have to find a way that works for you. You get to decide how you want to transition to your own thing, and you can move at your own pace. It's helpful to set a goal of when you want to leave your job. All of my experiences have been rich in their unique ways. Yet the skills that I am most thankful for that help me daily as an entrepreneur are Sales, Customer Service, and Organization.

Brand Ambassador and Sales

If you have no sales, you have no business, said, everyone! Literally. If you are not generating sales, your business is out of business. You cannot operate a business without sales. This fact is why you must learn how to sell before you become a business owner. Learn how to sell to customers *before* you have the pressure of selling your goods or services for a living. Before I started working for myself, I worked in careers that helped improve my ability to sell. One of those positions was Brand Ambassador. Brand ambassador work is an excellent practice for future entrepreneurs because you learn how to represent a brand. Representing other brands will teach you how to represent your brand.

A brand ambassador is the face of a company. They educate the public about new product services or ideas. Brand ambassadors also can collect useful client data through surveys for companies; brand ambassadors can conduct product demos and sell products to customers. I started doing brand ambassador work in 1996. My first job was a promo for the Tyra Banks "Got Milk" Campaign. I have over 24 years of brand ambassador work experience. In 2016, I retired from doing brand ambassador work for other companies. Within a 24-year timeframe, I'd already worked with several well-known national and international Fortune 500 companies. I'd worked several events and tradeshows and raised several millions of dollars at charity auctions. The more opportunities I took to represent various brands at tradeshows and events, the more I expanded my ability to sell anything.

Brand ambassador work is unique because it varies. One job may consist of taking surveys. The next promotional job may consist of selling wine to customers at a grocery store. Jobs like this are great for learning how to sell goods and services. I practiced selling whether or not the job had a physical product to sell. For example, sometimes, as a brand ambassador, my job would be to collect names, phone numbers, email addresses, and physical addresses. Do you know how much of a salesperson you have to be (at a booth) to get people's attention? To get them to listen to your offer and then get them to give their name, phone number, email, and address? Do you know how much of a salesperson you have to be to get the attention of someone at a fair with lots of alcohol to do a survey? You have to be a hell of a convincing and a damn good salesperson. There are certainly opportunities for brand ambassadors to work on job assignments that sell products to customers. I did all of the above. Either way, you learn how to sell to the customer because you learn how to listen to them and meet their needs. You become a master at interacting with people and uncovering how your product can help them. Notice I said, *your product.*

What I love about brand ambassador work is that it puts you in front of people talking about a product, service, or idea. It's great practice! Talking to customers face-to-face is an excellent way to educate your customers and land a sale. This activity is what you are going to have to do as a business owner. Talking to people face-to-face is what builds trust. As a business owner, you may struggle at the beginning when you ask customers to buy your product. You may even struggle with talking about your product. Nervousness is common to all business owners. Brand ambassador work teaches you to get past your fears. The more you talk to people, the more quickly you will get over your fears. You have to talk to people to discover who they are, what they need, and how you may be able to meet that need. These are all fact-finding questions that open the door to you learning more about the customer, ultimately leading to a sale.

Law Enforcement and Customer Service

Remember, in the last section, when I said that without sales, you have no business? Well, without customers, you have no company. Hello somebody? It does not matter how wonderful your product is if no one is buying it. When you are blessed to acquire a customer, you want to keep them. Ideally, you want to create a lifetime customer. I suggest sharpening your customer skills before you become a business owner, if you are already in business you can benefit from this advice as well. My most challenging customer service jobs helped me grow as an entrepreneur. And nothing was more challenging than being a cop. I chose to become a Federal cop twice in my life. I also worked for an armed security company. Police officers are supposed to protect and serve the public. There are so many rules to follow, for the safety of officers and the safety of customers.

Good customer service as a cop means paying attention to details and staying alert to hazards. I had to learn how to win people over with my personality. Some people wouldn't give me a chance simply because I wore a uniform. Typically, in a career like law enforcement, no one likes you, but everyone needs you. People can be very rude simply because you were dispatched, meaning that someone called the police, and you showed up. I was trained that no matter how people behaved, I had to remain in control and calm.

I learned how to deal with irate customers by listening and using verbal judo. The lack of good customer service could result in injury or worst. Your customers are people who you strive to keep safe, and they count on you! A good police officer is one that has exceptional customer service. They are reliable, trustworthy, and have good character. As a Federal officer, I polished valuable skills like how to listen to customers, identifying their issues, resolving complaints, and delivering customer satisfaction. Customer satisfaction for me as a law enforcement officer was when the public was happy with the presence of safety that I added to the community.

An officer is another part of the community, just like the firefighter, and the teacher. Each one is valuable and can add to the community when they do their jobs with integrity. I earned love and respect quickly on my police tours. People had to get to know me beyond my uniform. They had to see my smile. You have to learn how to attract people as a business owner. You attract customers with your charisma and reliable services. Customers can be challenging to acquire and keep.

First of all, you have to attract your customers and get their attention long enough to show them what you are selling. They want to know quickly that your services work. In law enforcement, an officer is a servant of the public; their image should be one of integrity, reliability, and authority. An officer's presence is the first line of security. That's why so much care goes into grooming and the uniform. As an officer, your image and your actions are held to a high standard. I got written up once for not wearing my tie with my winter uniform! People who call cops for help hope the officers are going to be true to their oath of serving and protecting. People are trusting you, sometimes to save their lives! I felt responsible for everyone and everything during my watch. I wanted to be there when people needed me the most. An officer is expected to be true to their word and do what he or she said they did. You could get in serious legal trouble for lying. In business, customers want to know that they can count on you to deliver consistently. Can they rely on you, to tell the truth?

Law Enforcement gave me service skills. It taught me how to work and talk to people to get results, with minimal drama. I learned how to be a mediator and listen to all sides of a story before reaching conclusions. Law enforcement taught me to check for facts. Learning this skill helps me listen better to my customers. I learned how to work with people from all backgrounds, religions, genders, cultures, and ethnicities. You learn empathy if you are a good cop. You see yourself in others. This skill translates into business. When I create products or services, I only create products I would want and products that interest me. My target audience are people who share the same interest.

I like creating products that I wish I had when I was starting out as an entrepreneur, like this book. Products that I know will resonate and add value because they come from real-life experience. I learned how to be relatable and resonate with people as a police officer. In hindsight, this resonance arrived from a place of refusing to allow my uniform to outshine my presence and personality. I had a poker face when it was time to have a poker face. You have to know timing in business as well. I got to know people on my tours. They became my friends.

In business, my customers are people who I share valuable information with and make their lives better. I learned a lot about customer service during my Federal law enforcement years; in such an extreme position, customer service becomes critical for success. I loved being a cop because I learned how to communicate with customers from all backgrounds. Can you communicate with people from all faiths, genders, sexual orientations, and nationalities? Any job that forces you to deal directly with people and serve them is helpful because it will build your endurance and customer service skills. You will learn in real-time how to handle demanding situations and how to work with people.

Administration and Organization

Being organized will keep you sane and help you run your business as smoothly as possible. You can't keep up with your day-to-day business operations if you are not organized. Jobs that sharpen your organizational abilities will benefit you as a business owner. Working as an administrative assistant helped me develop my organizational skills. As an assistant, I consistently received assignments and projects to juggle. When I didn't have work to do, I made up work. I used some of my downtime to create systems that kept me organized. The organization of my time helped me to complete my tasks quicker. As an assistant, I was once responsible for timekeeping for over 30 employees paid bi-weekly. Employees were on-call, sometimes they worked overtime, and they could change their schedules at a moment's notice. New employees were continually coming on-board at the same time old employees were out-processing. Employees could share their time off with each other, and request various types of leaves of absence.

I went out of my way to make sure that I was available to answer payroll questions. I made last-minute critical changes, like adding overtime that an employee submitted after the payroll deadline or processing a new last-minute employee. I was always the one on the phone, speaking directly to my payroll contact. I was always there to hit the submit button, ready to edit and resubmit the payroll if changes were needed. I planned my vacations around my payroll responsibilities. Payroll was a job in itself.

I had to create a system to keep up with the madness of it all. And that's exactly what entrepreneurs have to do. Sometimes, they have to get creative. The best way to manage a stressful workload is to create a step-by-step system to deal with each challenge at hand. I had to mastermind what steps I was going to take to make sure that people were getting paid on time, primarily because I was responsible. I didn't want people not to get paid because of a step I missed. When your business is not organized, you miss steps in the process. I had to create a systematic process that I could teach to a back-up assistant. A back-up is someone that can take your place and do your work if you are absent.

My job as an admin taught me how to organize paperwork, people, and events. It gave me a sense of accountability. The type of obligation that a business owner would feel. I learned to manage my workload and others' workloads by creating systems that kept me organized. I had to be able to find every file and record at a moment's notice. I had to show compliance and be able to track paperwork sent out for approval signatures (sometimes, this paperwork would circulate for months, throughout the facility, before signature approval). Are you currently working for someone else, goddess? Look around, what skills are you learning now that will help you as a business owner? Sharpen those skills now, and you will thank me later when you are running your 6 and 7 figure businesses.

These positions taught me to keep track of ongoing projects, project status, and project reporting deadlines. I was also accountable for keeping track of all policies, making sure that the policies were reviewed and updated a year from creation. I ensured that new policies followed specific protocols before being written into official policy. Excel sheets and color coordinating became my friend. Excel is still my friend today. Being an Admin gave me the secretarial and technical skills I use now to work my business. Working as an admin sharpened my leadership skills, which still helps me as a business owner. Working a position where you are responsible for keeping up multiple workloads can help you remain organized. Working in an area of leadership where you are responsible for someone else will keep you on your toes and prepare you for managing people. I am glad I had the chance to do assistant work while working in the government. The government requires attention to detail. Running a successful business requires your attention to detail. The better organized you are, the better your chances for business success.

This section addressed how African American women business owners benefit from developing her sales, customer service, and organization skills. You may develop these skills from either work or non-work-related experiences. As you prepare yourself, you develop your business. While you are on your way to becoming an entrepreneur full-time, and as you grow, you must take every opportunity, you can to develop your knowledge. When I worked for others, I learned everything I could and took advantage of every training offered.

I remained teachable to those who had something that I wanted to learn. This is the way that you give yourself an advantage. Take every opportunity that makes sense for your growth and advancement. This strategy is one that any entrepreneur can use. It is pivotal to see the value of being right where you are. Using your job to make you better will keep you from feeling stuck while you work. I want to encourage you even if you are working for someone else while planning your exit. You can grow right where you are planted. You can develop your business idea in the middle of heaven or hell!

All businesses start with one idea. You can build your dream and learn from your 9 to 5 role. You can learn how to take advantage of any opportunity that adds to your experience and helps you grow as an entrepreneur. You can use working for someone else as a steppingstone to achieving your goals; you can learn while you work and develop your business.

Develop Your Knowledge

Business research suggests that African American female entrepreneurs display positive attitudes toward training and research when compared to White female entrepreneurs[57]. African American female business owners actively seek opportunities to increase their business knowledge to advance themselves within their entrepreneurial ventures. The lack of business education and professional guidance, due to the lower socioeconomic backgrounds, was noted by Garrett-Scott as a hindrance to African American entrepreneurs in the 19th century. It was evident within my business study that African American women worked consistently to increase their business knowledge.

African American female entrepreneurs used outside employment as a platform to develop their entrepreneurial field and product knowledge. They made business research a continuous process. These two core themes, discovered through my research, had not yet been identified within the literature concerning African American female entrepreneurs. Establishing a continuous process of conducting business research is essential for the development of African American female-owned businesses. Ongoing business research by African American women shortens the learning curve and helps them to become successful. Survey respondents repeatedly stressed the need for all business owners, specifically African American women business owners, to research business-related subjects consistently. This research should take place throughout the entrepreneurial journey;

respondents noted that it is especially crucial at the business start-up phase. I asked if participants conducted research before starting their businesses. All the participants had researched information before starting their businesses. One respondent clarified in her response to a question about what advice participants would give to African American women business owners:

> African American female business owners should be open to any type of changes that may come their way; they have to be on top of their business. They should do their research and be ahead of everyone else within their field. (R01)

My education in business started in 2007 when I opened my first official business. I learned from a mixture of hard knocks and academic education. Fast forward to 2020, two books written, and several companies started. Within a business, there are many ways to enhance your knowledge. The best education is hands-on training. You have to get out there and start working in your business. Experience is the best teacher. African American women business owners can also shorten their business learning curve by attending conferences and taking courses.

Conferences

Conferences are great opportunities to get information, network, and learn. A conference is a gathering of members of the same business or field of expertise. Attending conferences helped me to expand my business knowledge and remain current and knowledgeable with business trends. There are several types of conferences. I recommend attending workshops, consumer shows, and conventions to develop your business knowledge. Workshops are educational. They take place with a small group of people who converse on practices and skills that are particular to an industry. Workshops generally consist of specialists within a specific field who come together, interact, and discuss what they've learned. As a business owner, just starting out, you may not be considered as an expert within your field.

Nonetheless, if you want to be an expert, you have to hang around experts. People who put together conferences know that *wannabe successful* business owners want to connect to *already successful* business owners. You want to connect to people who are where you want to be, who have the type of success that you envision within your company. Some conferences, especially business-to-business conferences, offer attendees an opportunity to pay extra to attend networking events.

Conferences can also be consumer shows or conventions. Consumer shows are shows that are open to the public for a fee. Consumer shows are also called tradeshows, exhibitions, and expos; the shows offer a collection of products and services in a specific field or industry. Conventions are events usually held annually. Conventions also display products and have keynote speakers within a particular field of interest like consumer shows. Conventions either have a professional focus or are fan-inspired. I recommend that business owners attend professional conventions to get a broad perspective of their industry.

My favorite conferences to attend are ones that have multiple presenters and various business topics. I like learning in this type of environment because it's laid back and pressure-free. I get to sit back, drink coffee, watch presentations, and take notes. I can use my notes as a later reference. Some conferences give you a copy of all the lectures along with handouts. This method provides information that you may use to build on your business education.

Conferences are like attending a workshop on steroids. You often get the chance to meet and connect to other entrepreneurs who may have services that can help your business and vice versa. Usually, the conference presenters are considered knowledgeable in their field, which is what qualifies them to teach in a conference setting. They may have a formula to share with the audience that they implemented in their business. At conferences, you typically learn secret methods from people who have done the work. It is wise to attend conferences that educate you on topics that you want to learn more about *and* conferences that can help your business develop. One of the best times to attend a conference is when you are preparing to launch a product or service because you can do your research while you develop your idea. You may discover valuable information at the conference that you can incorporate into your business. You never know who you are going to meet at the event, and what type of unexpected advice you may gain. You may also find out at an event if your business idea is solid or if it needs tweaking. At a smaller business-to-business venue with keynote speakers, you may get the opportunity to connect with leaders within a specific industry.

Keynote speakers are more accessible at smaller venues because there are smaller crowds and fewer people waiting in line to talk to the keynote speaker. You may even sit at a table with a keynote speaker and not know it! That happened to me at a conference that my partner and I attended while we were creating our first CBD brand. We happened to be sitting at the same table as the CEO of an international clothing brand. I introduced myself to him and found out during the conference that he was one of the main presenters at the event! His bio was very impressive, to say the least, as the CEO of over 30 companies, and a generator of billions of dollars in sales. It was an honor. The conference was three days long, and for three days, I sat at the same table with a branding expert, who was also a keynote speaker. At the time, my partner and I were working on solidifying our logo design with our designer. We were able to get lots of great free feedback from an expert who had already generated billions. As a result of incorporating his advice, we gained more clarity on the direction of our brand. We went on to create a successful CBD company. Conferences can be your classroom where you conduct additional business research, gather information, and absorb valuable knowledge.

Business Schools and Online Classes

It is no secret that African American women love school. We love propelling ourselves forward and learning all that we can about a subject. We love achieving academic success because often, for many of us, it means overcoming multiple challenges while being the first in our families to obtain degrees. We love knowing how to do something. Education gives us our fundamentals, and for some of us, it makes us feel a little more confident because we are, at least, armed with theoretical information.

The most useful business schools for African American female business owners go beyond academic knowledge. The schools teach tested information that you can apply to help you to develop your business. Ideally, these are quick bite-size courses that get right to the point and immediately provide solutions and information for the busy entrepreneur. Bite-size courses are courses for the African American woman who is too busy running her business to go for another master's degree. Regardless, she needs critical information on *how* to actually run her business. I offer online courses that keep African American female entrepreneurs moving forward, at every level of their business development.

Business development is multitiered and multilayered. It requires lots of strategic planning and going with the flow. It starts the moment you decide you want to become a business owner and continues throughout the duration of your company. Fun is dreaming about what you wish to achieve and creating a road map to help you get there. Fun is in surrendering when things are out of your control and going on an adventure. Business development is the framework in which you create your business, like an artist, you craft your company. Your business may start with one idea and branch out into many. Some ideas will make it, and some ideas will not be as successful. As you develop your business, you will learn to try different business ideas to see which one brings you the highest return on your investment.

Key 4: Money Matters: Financial Wizardry

Speaking of investment. It takes money to run a business in most cases. Entrepreneurs frequently fund their businesses to get them going. This money may come from their employment within the traditional workforce, credit cards, or personal savings account[11]. Every research participant stressed the need for African American female entrepreneurs to be prepared to fund their own business whenever possible. This advice emerged, partly due to the difficulty of obtaining capital for African American female business owners. I asked what challenges they faced as African American female business owners that were perhaps not faced by White business owners. R05 responded, "Acquiring money is a challenge; I think so.... As an African American female business owner, I often I have to pay right then and there, there is no grace period." The difficulty of obtaining a loan for African American female business owners coupled with the lack of financial support from a two-person household income, make it paramount for a successful African American female entrepreneur to become financially savvy and able to fund her business using her own resources. The color of your skin can either help you, hurt you, or not affect you at all. Racism does exist, and systems need to change to benefit all entrepreneurs.

Business numbers don't lie and people like money. If you establish a rapidly growing business with steady sales on the books, you are going to be hard to ignore! Regardless of color. Your business performance will speak loudly, and it will be challenging to keep denying you. It is possible to *make* people recognize you by becoming extremely good at what you do and showing

112

that within your spreadsheet numbers and your satisfied customers. Buyers looking to acquire companies, typically don't care what ethnicity you are. Remember, sometimes, this, too, can work out in your favor. Buyers want to know: how many sales do you have on the books? They want to know about the professionalism of your business and if your company performs well financially. To achieve business success, African American women have to be vested financially in their business. I asked women business owners if they had any advice for African American women desiring to start their own businesses.

R03 suggested, "For the first couple of years in business she should take the money and put it back in the business. Do not go on a shopping spree; just take the money and put it back into the business." This advice means you must also be fiscally responsible. You have to invest in yourself first. We cannot expect someone else to pour into us financially what we are not willing to pour into ourselves with our own energy. This reality is true for any business owner. The world is not always going to be a fair place. It might not be right, but this is a fact as long as beings continue to see themselves as separate from the whole and each other.

A financially solid woman is going to have more options available to her than a woman who is viewed as financially irresponsible. African American women, in particular, need to become extra savvy and learn how to play the money game like everyone else. You have to play the money game to win. What is the money game? The game of making money. Before you start playing the money game, you have to remove the blockages you may have about money. Before you can be successful from a financial standpoint within your business, you are going to have to tap into abundance, energy, and manifestation. This fourth key is especially important because this is where I've had the most revelations and where I've experienced the most growth. I became exceptionally financially savvy throughout the years of becoming an entrepreneur. I've grown leaps and bounds through trial and error. Tapping into a formula I call, AEM, Abundance, Energy, and Manifestation has been instrumental in providing the esoteric framework for financial breakthroughs within my businesses.

A is for Abundance

Money is Abundance. The world is abundant. You have everything you need. Abundance is all around you. Abundance may not seem readily available within the form you wish to have. Yet, one look at a field of lilies during the springtime will tell you that abundance takes many forms. To attract financial success as a business owner, I had to capture the vibration of abundance first. I had to feel abundant. I had to acknowledge everything I had (*already*). This acknowledgment of gratitude helps you to feel abundant and attract more abundance. This condition is what is meant by the saying, "gratitude opens the door to abundance."

I discovered that you can't manifest what you don't believe you already have. Let me repeat that, you can't manifest what you don't already have. You have to capture the vibration of the state or condition that you want, how it makes you feel, *and* how it makes others feel. You conjure up feelings of abundance by being mindful of what you have and by visualizing the successful outcomes and client satisfaction from your business services. When I wanted to grow my business and target my services toward women, I started visualizing myself helping people, specifically women. I started feeling what it would feel like emotionally, to help someone heal mentally, physically, and spiritually. Whatever project I do or plan to do, I imagine myself doing the project and the feelings of joy that come along with helping people and making money. This practice helps me to attract a sense of wealth that leads to physical manifestation.

My relationship with abundance improved once I started believing that the Universe was on my side and that all my needs were already met. These are life lessons that I was reminded of throughout my entrepreneurial journey. You have to believe in the seemingly impossible. There will be times you may struggle to pay your bills. Being able to see abundance all around you when everything you built feels threatened will take courage and faith. Feeling the liveliness of abundance will help you during challenging times. There are ways to cultivate the feeling of plenty. I like playing music and dancing! These actions always make me feel good.

E is for Energy

Money is energy and energy flows. It tends to go where it is wanted and needed. Money is a feminine energy. It likes to be valued, appreciated, and, yes, loved. Loving money? Usually, it's that last piece of the sentence that trips us up. Especially if you had a religious upbringing, you might think that money is evil. Money is neither good nor bad. Money is what you make of it; more importantly, what you do with it. Are you an entrepreneur who has a tough time charging for your services? You may feel guilty about asking for the sale of your own products! This feeling is actually normal; I've seen it with my own clients.

Sometimes people get shy around money. Some of these reasons are hidden in the subconscious mind, again coming from childhood. I teach my clients how to explore the root of their suspicions about money and learn to face those fears. The fear of money is an anxiety you must overcome because if you don't, you will sabotage your business success. Sometimes your issue is receiving and learning how to receive. Maybe you don't feel worthy? Often when you are "extra responsible," it's easy to put yourself on the "backburner" and do everything and be everything for everyone. You may be the one that's always giving, and the moment someone wants to give to you, you reject the offer. Why did you reject the offer? Because you have money issues, and the way you feel about money may affect your business's ability to be financially wealthy. If you don't have good thoughts about money and welcome it, then money is not going to want to be around you or your business.

Money flows where it is wanted and valued. Again, money is energy. Another thing that money isn't attracted to is jealousy. Specifically, when you hate other people who have more money than you simply because they have more money than you. Money does not flow with the energy of jealousy. When you are jealous of someone's financial success, in essence, you are sending signals that "there is not enough money available to bless you, too." If you have been doing your due diligence and laying fertile seeds, then you know it's merely a matter of time before you see an increase in your wealth. You have to believe it can happen for you, too! Get internally excited when you see a rich person. Before you used to talk bad about rich people, now you shake their hand, walk up to them, and introduce yourself! If you secretly hate rich people, you will not be rich. And it takes money to help people. Rich people keep the economy going and provide employment. Your money energy flows deep and is connected to your womb, a receiver, and a creator. Human beings can have several blockages within their bodies that prohibit maximum wealth flow. The universe will continue to repel money from you until you pluck the energetic root of poverty, which is often hate, fear, and abandonment.

In 2007 when I started my business adventures, I didn't fully know that you could either attract or repel money by the thoughts you had about money. Fortunately, I always had pretty healthy thoughts about money. Yet, I was still stuck. It took years to get past middle-class thinking. There is nothing right or wrong with any classification, middle-class, rich, or poor; it's all about your personal goals. *The Secrets of a Millionaire Mind* book was instrumental in my awakening about money. The book shared how rich people think versus how poor people think. There is a difference. I'd realized that although I knew how to attract money into my life, the amount I attracted was based on my ability to believe and receive. I was making money, but I was not a millionaire in 2012. I had to teach myself how to dream big. You may have to explore your attitudes about money. Depending on your culture, and the way you were raised, you may find that your beliefs about money are similar to your parents' ideas about money. This conditioning may help or hinder your perception. Within my exploration of African American women entrepreneurs and their thoughts about money, I've discovered that some women feel guilty about being rich. They feel guilty about receiving payment, and they feel guilty about charging for their services. Subconsciously some African American women feel that money is wicked.

M is for Manifestation

Manifestation is bringing into physical reality the energy of money. One way of manifesting money consciousness is to start hanging around people who have money. I realized that the more people I spent time with who were financially wealthy, the more their vibration would fine-tune my vibration. All things have a vibration, including people who have broken the curse of lack. I took notes and studied my rich friends. When I was ready to manifest money, I started associating myself with people who surpassed my personal financial goals. I needed to start thinking more like a rich businesswoman, not like a middle-class businesswoman. Again, more money does not equal better or worse.

When you surround yourself with people who run their own eight-figure businesses, you quickly learn what to do and what not to do with your money. You also learn what it takes to run an eight-figure and beyond business. I have been blessed to have friends who are self-made millionaires and billionaires. I've had the honor of seeing behind the scenes and day-to-day operations. I've also had the honor of working with them. I knew their money didn't make them better or worse. All of my extremely wealthy friends are givers and love to help people. The information they share is priceless and helps my finances.

In my experience, rich people do not come from a place of lack. They are givers, and they give. They want to teach you what they did to get where they are. They want to share their secrets. There is more within their creative minds that they have yet to release. They believe in the power of manifesting and attracting what you want into your life. I'll never forget when an eight-figure friend of mine invited my business partner and me to a meditation event regarding money. When my friend initially asked me, I recall telling my partner, when a multimillionaire invites you to attend a meditation event about money, you go. I attended the meeting, ready to learn.

I discovered that money is always there for the bold who believe they are worthy to receive it. Sometimes before we believe we can have something; we have to know that we deserve that very thing that we desire. Once you know what you want, and you know that you deserve it, the universe may inspire you with creative ideas to make money and/or put people in your life that bless you financially. You can be blessed in ways beyond what's normal. I've had people literally give me several thousands of dollars just because they wanted to give me money. I've also had ideas pop into my head in the middle of the night that led to financial success. You manifest money in uniquely creative ways. Hanging around friends who are wealthy and financially successful within their businesses helps you to see the varied ways one can accumulate wealth. This information can be helpful if you allow yourself to absorb your surroundings.

People who are successful will inspire you to do the same. Their actions will motivate you to keep reaching for your financial goals. They will remind you that it is possible to make lots of money and show you what it looks like to do such. They will inspire you to manifest your own money and show you *how to* be rich.

Financial Literacy

Financial capital is a key to business success and expansion; without money, the business owner stands a higher chance of failure.[4] African American women are the least likely group to apply for credit because of fear of rejection. African American female business owners experienced greater credit rejection compared to another minority and nonminority female entrepreneurs[45]. The study participants were aware of the need for capital to fund their businesses. They were also aware of the difficulty in securing capital from banks.

Four out of five (80%) of the participants in the study were single and divorced. A single-family household income may not produce as much as a married household income. Household revenue can be used as leverage to increase net worth, for start-up business cost, and loan collateral.[24] On average, African American household earnings are significantly less than White household incomes.[3] All participants within the study encouraged African American female entrepreneurs to develop financial capital necessary to fund their businesses themselves and to become financially invested in their business. In the 1800s, obtaining money for African American entrepreneurial ventures proved extremely difficult.[14] Not much has changed since 1899 when Du Bois suggested that African American business owners pour their own capital into their businesses. African Americans are still encouraged to be financially vested in their companies.[42]

Financial literacy is critical to business success. Financial literacy is getting a handle on your finances. I must share a secret that I don't know why no one tells business owners. Before you start your business, you want to become a master of your personal finances. Firstly, this gets you into the practice of watching your numbers. And as a business owner, you work with numbers in many aspects of your business. Secondly, it teaches you responsibility. You have to know how much money is going out (expenses) and what's coming in (sales). When you start managing the money you have within your personal account, it's like telling the universe that you can handle more. When you send out signals to the universe that you are grateful for what you have been given by managing it, you open the doors to receive more. Once you start your business, you may initially be doing your own accounting. Practice with your personal bank account will help you create the habit of looking at bank statements—a job you want to do even when you have an accountant. You want to keep an eye on the flow of your money so that surprises do not catch you. Again, I am speaking from experience here!

Keeping your personal finances in order is also beneficial to your credit. Getting a handle on your finances early also means getting a handle on your debt. You want to open a business ideally with good credit and debt-free. This advice is not to say you cannot have a successful business and bad credit. Still, your chances improve for loans when you have good credit and an excellent financial history. You don't want to give anyone any damn reason not to give you a loan. Make them work! You want creditors to tell you *Yes* because you have all of your shit together.

Ideally, before you start a business, you want to have some money saved up. You don't want to *be broke* and attempting to start a business. You want to have ready access to cash. You don't want to have to rely on your business sales to keep you afloat financially week-by-week. Ideally, you want to have enough money to take care of your basic needs. If you can manage to save enough money for one-to-two years' worth of your personal bills, then you will have so much stress lifted from you. Having money reserved will keep you from making desperate business deals to bring in needed capital. It often will take several months before you see a sale, and most business owners don't see a profit within their first few years of business. Can you imagine having the stress of waiting to see a profit in your business and not having any money to pay your personal bills?

Make sure your basic needs are taken care of before you go into business. Most business owners go into business and have a great idea that they think is going to start making them money right away. And it might! Then again, it might not. You want to be prepared either way. You have to be prepared if your business doesn't sustain you financially for a few years. Expecting your business to meet your day-to-day financial needs immediately can be a disaster because it causes stress. If you don't get paid, you don't eat. You want to have another source of income to help you take care of yourself while you build your business.

Business Funding Options

Let's say you can take care of your basic financial needs, but you have no money to start your business. Or perhaps you're like most eager entrepreneurs, and you want to start a business, but you have limited-to-no capital. Do you have options? Yes, of course, there are options for people who want to start a business with limited funds. In fact, many successful entrepreneurs built their businesses with limited funds. You can start a business with no money! Start a blog, for example. The most crucial ingredient to be a successful entrepreneur is passion. If you have passion, then you will find a way out of no way to live your entrepreneurial dream. There are also funding options to consider. There are also specific options for women of color, which I will discuss later within this section.

Shoestring budget. One of the easiest ways to fund your business is to use the shoestring budget model to build a successful business. The shoestring budget model means to put only minimal capital (the money that is absolutely required) to run your business and reach successful outcomes. The key, however, is that you must have a budget even if you start with fifty bucks. Working with a shoestring budget can be both challenging and fun. Often you are working with your own money.

If you have limited to no funds, you want to look at how much money you have and what kind of business you can start with minimal funds. Online businesses that don't require too much overhead can be an excellent place to start a company. A quick Google search will give you a list of businesses that you can enter for minimal capital investment. Start a business that you can afford to start from where you are financially right now. Start asking, what kind of business can you start now, right where you are, that won't strain your pocketbooks? The key to successful bootstrapping is to work within your financial means. You may decide to start a blogging business, or maybe you can afford to open a retail store. It does not matter what kind of business it is, as long as it resonates with you, and you can afford to get it started. To bootstrap like a pro, you have to know:

1. How much personal cash flow you have per month?
2. How much it costs to run your business monthly?
3. Your personal expenses.
4. Your business's expenses (listed by priority).
5. How much of your personal income can you afford to put toward your company each month?

It would be wise to create a budget for your business; this activity will keep you aware of financial obligations. You will be less likely to be caught by surprise expenses, and you will always know where you stand financially. When you bootstrap your business, you take pride in investing in yourself. You learn to put the money you earned back into the business so that it builds. You have to have realistic growth expectations for your company because, with a limited budget, you may not immediately see results. Your business sales may develop and increase as you add to your financial capital and build your business.

Family friends/Crowdfunding. You can always ask those who are close to you for money. This choice is not always the best option, but it may be necessary if you are low on funds. I wouldn't suggest outright asking without some form of business plan or presentation. A business plan will let your family and friends know that you take your business and their money seriously. It will make them more likely to invest in you. A business plan will show them how their money can help you grow. Sometimes it is easier to ask people you know for money, especially when they know your character is trustworthy. At the same time, you don't have to limit your asking to family and friends.

You can take advantage of the ease of technology and start a crowdfunding campaign online. A Google search will identify several crowdfunding platforms. Research the right platform for you and ask for support. Kiva loans are an example of a community driven crowdfunding service. The people who work at Kiva are on a mission to provide capital to businesses owners who find it difficult to access funding[63]. Crowdfunding will let you know if you have a viable business concept that people are interested in supporting. Asking for money from strangers, in general, will prepare you for asking for sales from your customers later. You will build courage while practicing your elevator pitch. Crowdfunding is cool because the concept, in general, creates a sense of community. People can potentially become involved with what you do and support you. The people that help you start your business may also become your customers. The key to asking for money is to be clear about why the money is needed and how you will use the funds.

Credit card. Using a credit card to help fund your business is an old method of securing capital. This method is not ideal, but it can work. Using a credit card to fund your business is exactly what it sounds like, you use the money on your credit card to finance your business. This method should only be used if you already use credit responsibly. You will have to be disciplined, organized, and strategic to stay on track with payments and also to ensure you are not maxing out your cards. Some entrepreneurs will advise you to max out your cards to start a business. I don't suggest this approach because it can negatively affect your credit score. Credit card funding can be a benefit for a short period, or as a supplement to other funding you've acquired. Credit cards can get you out of a pinch, and help you purchase essential items for your business. Some banks which offer business accounts to their clients also provide business credit cards to their customers. Securing a business bank credit card may less of a hassle if you are already a business client with your bank. If you have a good reputation with your bank, this type of credit or loan may be available to you as an option.

SBA loan. The Small Business Administration offers several funding options for small business owners. The money comes from lenders within their network. The SBA sets money to the side specifically for Women-Owned Small Business (WOSB) within underrepresented firms[62].
The SBA offers several types of financing from start-up loans for new business owners to commercial mortgages when you get ready to buy, build, expand, or remodel your business. The SBA also offers equipment financing, credit card, term loans, and lines of credit.

Grants. I love grants because you typically don't have to pay them back, and grants can cater to the applicant's needs. There are several types of business grants. There are grants for women business owners, veterans' business grants, female veteran grants. The Federal government offers programs to Native American small business owners and other minority groups, yet not African American women, unfortunately. However, there are plenty of business grants within the private sector that cater specifically to African American business owners. There are also start-up business grants. The Minority Business Development Agency has an annual grant competition. There are grants for everyone and for every aspect of your business. Grant providers make their offers to various demographics. There are grants where anyone is encouraged to apply, and grants targeted to underserved groups like women, military veterans, and minority entrepreneurs.

The guidelines to qualify for a grant is contingent on the grant's rules. Each grant will have its stipulations spelled out. The qualification process to meet the grant's requirements is often tedious and competitive because it's usually free money! Although cumbersome, it may be worth it! I suggest enlisting the aid of a close friend or mentor to help you sort through and find appropriate grants. It can be time-consuming to search and apply for the funds. At least by enlisting a friend, you can apply and know that you're already qualified.

Angel investor. Angel investors are another option for business owners to secure capital. An angel investor is an individual with a high net-worth that provides start-up capital typically in exchange for ownership, equity, or convertible debt in your company. A convertible debt occurs when a business owner borrows money from a lender, and both parties enter an agreement to repay all or part of the loan by converting a defined number of shares. Usually, angel investors are accredited investors, but this status is not a requirement.

An accredited investor is someone with assets of $1M, not including individual property, or someone with an earned income of $200K for two years, or a married couple with a combined income of $300K. Angel investors may finance your business once or continuously during its start-up phase. They typically invest in your business's early stages. They can help you get your doors open by providing money. They can also pour cash into your business to get it going. Angel investors invest in you, the entrepreneur; therefore, the loan terms for angel investors are usually more favorable when compared to loans from other lenders. However, because start-up loans are risky, Angel investors typically ask for a higher rate of return compared to traditional lenders. Often angel investors may be your friends or family. There are also angel networking platforms where angel investors pool their money together to invest.

Venture capital. Venture capitalists are another funding option for your new or growing business. The funding usually comes from a venture capital firm. Like angel investors, venture capital firms may finance your business in exchange for equity in the company. However, unlike angel investors, venture capitalists don't usually provide seed funding (or early start-up funding). Also, venture capitalists typically fund companies that are slightly more mature, with higher evaluations, and funding amounts. They may not be the best option for brand new businesses without a prior history. The company does not necessarily have to be profitable to be a candidate for venture funding. Both angel investors and venture capitalists are considered high-risk investors. Venture capital is regarded as a substantial risk because there is a chance that investors may lose their investment because of the risky nature of starting and running a business.

Angel investors are considered higher risk than venture capitalists because angel investors help businesses often in the very beginning (very fragile), stage of their business.

Microfinance. Microfinancing is typically a smaller, short-term loan with a low-interest rate. These loans are offered to self-employed individuals, new start-ups with minimal funding requirements, and small business owners. A microloan is typically no more than $50K. Nonprofit organizations are the most common microfinancers. Some of these organizations emphasize lending to women, minorities, veterans, and other underserved entrepreneurs who have historically had difficulty securing bank business loans. In addition to providing microloans, some microlenders offer free mentoring, assistance, and business training. The terms to qualify for a microloan are often less stringent than a bank's requirements, and the process to qualify is less time-consuming. Microfinancing is also a great way to build your business credit.

Note on Investors

Outside investors are a fantastic way to fund your business. Whether you get financed through a business or a personal loan, typically, investors want to know answers to the same questions. How much do you need? How will you use the money? When will they get the money back? How much money can you (potentially) make them (if the investor has equity)? How profitable is your idea? To attract an investor, it's better to have a business plan and a pitch deck. This requirement is a vital take-away from this section.

You can go online and create a professional business plan and a pitch deck. Include a year's worth of expenses within your pitch deck. Again, the investor will want to know how much money you need from them; therefore, it's better to ask for more money up-front than to have to ask for more money later. Your salary may be an expense. Even if they are interested in funding your business, investors don't want to pay for your personal bills. This fact is why it's best to start a business while you can sustain yourself financially. Sometimes scarcity is what fuels people to beat tremendous odds. Not having money can also be a blessing because it forces you to sell something! It forces you to do business. But why start a business when you are broke when you can plan early and start with money in the bank and less stress?

Know Your Numbers

Numbers are interesting. They make business owners nervous. The moment you mention numbers, people think, "math…there is something they need to know," and they "don't know it." Numbers intimidate the hell out of people, especially business owners. We think we have to be mathematicians when the reality is we do not. We don't have to have a Ph.D. in math to do business well. I *understand* why numbers intimidate so many. I, too, had to get past my fear of numbers within my business.

There are a few basics you must know to run your business effectively. And there are specific numbers you will want to know. First, you need to know how much money you want to make so that you can know exactly where to focus your selling efforts. Again, you must have a goal to reach. What is your desired profit? How much money would you like to make this year? How much money would you like to make this month? You also must know how much it costs to run your business, i.e., your expenses. It's essential that you know how much it costs to run your business all the way down to the two cents that it may cost you to add sprinkles to one cupcake. If you are shipping your products, shipping and package charges are part of your expenses. This money granularity will help you stay on track of your costs and not be taken off guard. It is said that if you don't know your numbers, then you don't know your business. You must have your mind on your money. Another group of numbers that you're going to want to know are your margins.

Argh, Margins!

In business accounting and finance, a profit margin is a measure of a company's earnings compared to its revenue. **Gross profit margin** (total revenue minus cost of goods sold (COGS)), **operating profit margin** (revenue minus COGS and operating expenses), and **net profit margin** (revenue minus all expenses, including interest and taxes) **are the three main profit margin metrics** used to determine business profitability. This section will cover each of the three metrics and provide a mock income statement sample with numbers to illustrate each formula.

Gross profit margin is the difference between how much it costs you, the owner, to create your product or service and how much you sell your product or service for. It is also known as the margin of sales or gross profit ratio. The gross margin is expressed as a percentage of revenue of the selling price. Your gross profit shows how much money is left over *after* you pay the cost of goods sold (COGS). The cost of goods sold is *the cost* to create your product/service, i.e., the direct costs of producing the goods sold by your company. This amount includes the cost of the materials and labor directly used to create the good. Your *cost* will *only* include *direct* costs to *produce* your products and services. How much will it cost you to *sell* your cupcakes, for example? Website development, monthly fees, computer systems, salaries, overhead costs, and marketing are **not** included within your gross profit margin. Those numbers are reflected within the operating margin and net profit margin for the business. The gross profit margin is calculated by subtracting the cost of goods sold (COGS) from total revenue and dividing that number by your total revenue. The top number in the equation, the gross profit or gross margin, is the total revenue minus the direct costs of *creating* that product or service. Again, direct costs (COGS) do not include operating expenses, interest payments, and taxes, among other things.

GROSS PROFIT MARGIN

$$\text{Gross Profit Margin} = \frac{(\text{Revenue} - \text{Cost of Goods Sold})}{\text{Revenue}}$$

For the sake of clarity, we will use the illustrations below for this section. Our company example is the Goddess Cupcake Boutique, an upscale cupcake boutique retail, an e-commerce business that sells custom cupcakes for celebrities. For example, let's say you own this upscale cupcake boutique. You generate $1 million in total revenue for the year, and your Cost of Goods sold (direct cost of materials) is $500K, this is how the numbers would look in the formula:

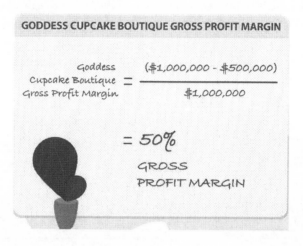

GODDESS CUPCAKE BOUTIQUE GROSS PROFIT MARGIN

$$\text{Goddess Cupcake Boutique Gross Profit Margin} = \frac{(\$1,000,000 - \$500,000)}{\$1,000,000}$$

$$= 50\% \text{ GROSS PROFIT MARGIN}$$

The gross profit margin percentage tells us that your Goddess Cupcake Boutique retains 50% of its revenues after the company pays the direct costs, like inventory. The gross profit in the example is $500K ($1 million in revenues minus $500K in COGS). The $500K you have remaining can be used for operating expenses and taxes.

Knowing your gross profit margin can help you analyze each sales transaction and identify which products are the most and least profitable for your business. This review will take the guesswork out of what products and services to sell. You can also calculate sales margins for group sales. For example, you may sell cupcake making education materials, cupcake tools, and cupcake boutique merchandise as a package deal to the customer. Calculating the sales margin for the entire package is proper because the bundle of the components represents the sale. Gross sales margins alone do not determine the profitability of your business. You must also know your operating profit margin.

Operating margin is how much profit your company makes per dollar of sales *after* paying for the costs of manufacturing. The cost of manufacturing may include salaries and raw materials. This number does not include your interest or taxes paid. The operating margin gauges your company's profitability. It identifies how much of each dollar of revenue remains *after* costs of goods sold *and* operational expenses are taken into consideration. Operational earnings are revenue minus the cost of goods sold, labor, and overall administrative cost that goes along with running a day-to-day business. Your operational earnings are earnings *before* interest and taxes. The operating margin is calculated by dividing your company's operating profit by its net sales.

Operating Margin = Operating Earnings / Revenue

Let's say the example below is your yearly income statement:

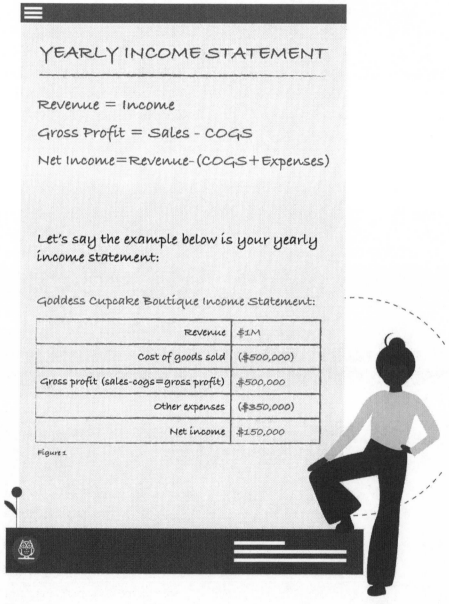

YEARLY INCOME STATEMENT

Revenue = Income

Gross Profit = Sales - COGS

Net Income = Revenue - (COGS + Expenses)

Let's say the example below is your yearly income statement:

Goddess Cupcake Boutique Income Statement:

Revenue	$1M
Cost of goods sold	($500,000)
Gross profit (sales-cogs=gross profit)	$500,000
Other expenses	($350,000)
Net income	$150,000

Figure 1

Figure 1

Goddess Cupcake Income Statement:
$1M Revenue
($500,000) Cost of Goods Sold (COGS)
$500,000 Gross profit (Sales - COGS = Gross Profit)
($350,000) Other expenses
$150,000 Net income (Total Expenses - Total Revenues = Net Income)

Using the information in Figure 1 and the operating margin formula, we can calculate that **Goddess Cupcake Boutique's** operating margin as the following:

Operating Margin = $150,000 / $1,000,000 = 0.15 or 15%

This result means that for every $1 in sales, the Goddess Cupcake Boutique makes $0.15 in operating earnings. What does all of this mean? Your operating margin shows the amount of revenue that's available to cover non-operating costs like interest. Investors and creditors like to see how a business is supporting itself. If your business can make enough money through its operations to sustain itself, you attract investors because you are a stable business and less risky. However, if your company requires both operating and non-operating income to cover the operation expenses, it shows that your business activity is unstable. This instability makes you look riskier to investors and creditors. The higher your operating margin, the more profitable your company appears. Profitability shows that your business is making enough money from its day-to-day operations to pay for its variable costs and fixed costs.

Net profit margin is the percentage of revenue that you have left *after* you have deducted all expenses from your sales. This number is also known as your bottom line or net margin. Your net profit shows the amount of profit your business extracts from its total sales. The net profit margin details *how much* of each dollar in revenue collected by your company renders into profit. This number is usually displayed as a percentage or decimal.

The formula for net profit margin is:

(Net profit ÷ Net sales) x 100 = Net profit margin

Let's consider the numbers in **Figure 1** to find the net profit. The revenue from selling cupcakes in 2020 is $1M, the cost of goods sold (direct cost of producing the cupcakes) is $500K, and all other operating expenses (including taxes and interest in this sample) are $350K. We can now calculate the gross and net profit margins for the Goddess Cupcake Boutique in 2020.

Based on the Income statement for the Goddess Cupcake Boutique:

Gross margin ($500K of gross profit divided by $1M of revenue) equals **50%**.

Net margin ($150K of net income divided by $1M of revenue) equals **15%**.

These numbers mean that after you pay your taxes, interest, and expenses, you have 15% of $1M remaining on your books. This value may not include your cash on hand. As we can see, there is a drastic difference between the gross margin and the net margin. You can't measure business profitability exclusively by the gross margin because selling, administrative overhead, expenses, interest, and taxes aren't included in the gross margin calculation. You want to know the net margin. Your net margin is the measurement you use to measure the overall financial profitability of your business. It's how much money you have left after you have paid your bills. A high-profit margin shows that your business has good expense control and adequate pricing. Depending on your industry and business, generally, an excellent profit margin is 10-20%.

If you don't know your numbers, you don't know your business. And you may end up making costly mistakes if you don't pay attention to expenses. Investors will not be attracted to you if you don't have a record of your numbers, especially your sales. You must show sales in your books. Your margins tell a story of lucrativeness.

Investing in Yourself

The most important investment is the one you make in yourself. You have a dream worth bringing to life. You can start investing in yourself now. If you want to grow your business, you may find scaling down in your personal life helpful. Get rid of the things you may not need like cable, and other subscriptions. Pay your bills down to make them manageable while you build your business. All business owners should pour their capital right back into their business. I call this recycling money because that's essentially what you're doing. You are taking money that you earned and using the money to fund your business. This action is smart finance. Recycling money into your business will take you farther than a *hood rich* mindset. Hood rich is acting and looking the part of someone with a luxurious lifestyle without accumulating real wealth. It's time to get past the hood rich mindset and grow your numbers. When you pour your money, time, and energy into your dream, you inspire the universe to open previously closed doors.

Faith in yourself and action is what is required to achieve success. Getting your credit and finances in order are action steps you can take now. If your personal finances are out-of-order and in disarray, it's going to be an extra task to stay on track financially within your business. If your personal finances are in shambles, it may affect your business. Having an awareness and knowledge of monies helps you become financially literate before you start your company. You can begin studying and investing in your business now. Money management is huge for business success!

Key 5: Networks of Support

It takes support to run a business. All the women I interviewed understood the importance of establishing networks of support[60]. A successful African American female entrepreneur was defined by a participant as someone who "connects with both African American female business owners and non-African American business owners in their area, for business support." I asked business owners what decisions they wished they had made differently during the start-up or maintenance of their business; the importance of support networks was again identified. "Yes, definitely. I wish I had more support or knew where to go to get the support.... I wish there was more assistance available for business owners." (R02)

The need for support networks is crucial for entrepreneurs in general. Women business owners are more likely to seek out the assistance of support groups compared to men.[10] The majority of the participants did not have strong family support systems or dependable formal networking systems in place[60]. However, they all agreed about the importance of having such systems. The systems established by the African American female entrepreneurs within the study emerged from the resources they had available. Their support systems were somewhat different from those of the White female business owners within the Reaves study[31]. They lacked strong family support and formal business organizational support. Instead, the participants incorporated self-support, positive people, and their faith within their networks of support.

Networking may provide business owners with additional tools, information, education, support, and contribute to their business growth.[10] Women in leadership positions benefit from both external and internal support. Family support, in particular, is listed as one of the factors that contribute to the success of women entrepreneurs[15]. This finding is huge. And this is why African American women must establish their own systems of support to be successful entrepreneurs. You have to be proactive and not reactive. Therefore, this final key is last, but not least.

I am going to share with you something I wish more people would tell entrepreneurs. You are going to need someone to lean on at some point within your entrepreneurial journey. Why? Because a man is not an island to himself. We require support from other human beings to aide in our growth. There are times when you will need assistance. You will need angels in human form to help you reach your goals. To be successful, you need resources; human capital is a resource. The final key to achieving business success is establishing reliable support networks.

When the Family is MIA

What do you do when your family is Missing in ACTION?

Women business owners, in general, thrive with supportive family units backing their decision to become entrepreneurs. Without direct family support, especially from a spouse, a female entrepreneur may not have enough financial or emotional support to become successful.

A single parent female entrepreneur may also have to cope with the challenge of managing family life and her business simultaneously. A challenging task. In my research, African American women continuously stressed that *it was just them*, so they had no choice but to make their business work. Sixty percent of study participants had the dual task of being a single parent and pursuing entrepreneurialism.

Eighty percent of the participants I studied indicated that they were divorced and single[60]. African American women, in general, are taking care of households, their children, and attempting to run a business with no support. There isn't anyone else there to help. And that's stressful.

Sometimes you may have family members around you, and you may (still) not feel supported by your own family. The lack of family support may act as a hindrance to female entrepreneurs, causing some to fail at their attempt to become business owners. "The lack of being encouraged to start [a] business is the first challenge for African American female entrepreneurs, the lack of encouragement from our families." This need for encouragement can extend to wanting approval from your family to live your dream. We can allow the lack of family approval to keep our businesses stagnant. Sometimes we allow family members who are not in business to dictate what we need to do or not do with our company. This relinquishment is madness, and it must stop. If you want business advice, first, stop asking family members who are not in business. And second, start hanging around business owners and seeking counsel from people you admire from a business standpoint. Your family is not automatically your business sounding board. They may not have the tools needed to help you.

Sometimes family members who are not in business may not understand the types of risks required for business owners to be successful. And they may discourage you from taking the business risks that you may need to take. Family can also be very discouraging if you don't reach success within their timeframe. They may give up on your business dreams, not realizing that there is no guaranteed timeframe for business success. Again, they may not understand because they are not business owners or in your shoes. An entrepreneur may not find their business sweet spot until several years of failing forward. Your family typically doesn't want you to fail. Your family loves you, and they don't want to see you suffer and make mistakes. Yet you have to be willing to fail if you're going to grow. You can't let the fears of others who aren't in business terrify you to the point of not taking a chance. Even if you have tried and failed many times, that's part of being a business owner. You must fail so you can grow. Fail often and fail fast. The more you fail, the closer you may be to success. This process is how you allow your failure to move you forward in business.

Not everything you do with your business is going to be acceptable to your family, and this is something you must acknowledge. It's not meant for your family to accept all things. They may not be capable. You have to know within yourself and have your own convictions. Sometimes merely starting a business and wanting to pursue your dreams is enough to make your family members misjudge you. It's 2020, and I am here to tell you that I have not always been supported in my business dreams. I am in the cannabis industry, and that has not always been welcomed with open arms. When you get into your creative space and you invent something unique, it might challenge the beliefs of those around you because they never heard of it!

There have been times when I shared my business dreams only to have them shot down by family who meant well. They didn't always understand or embrace my business uniqueness and my need to live my passion. The same may be true for you. This lack of understanding sometimes happens when you have revolutionary ideas that are not yet popular and mainstream. Often it is those closest to you (whose opinion you value the most) that hurt you the most (when they don't believe in your dream). At times people are afraid to back you because they are uncomfortable with what you're doing. And because they don't know what you're doing, it must be wrong. They bring their judgments, fears, and perceptions into your business in an attempt to control you. This activity often happens subconsciously. It is human nature, and nothing personal about you.

You have to remind yourself that entrepreneurs are often trailblazers who create paths where there were previously none! You may indeed be creating a blue ocean product or service that's ahead of its time, in the eyes of your family. As long as you are not harming others with your business, and you use wisdom, you have the right not to be placed in a box with your business ideas. You have the right to create a heart-centered legal business that you believe in—without interference from your family.

We reach out to our families because the world of entrepreneurialism is so lonely sometimes, that we search for that one close soul that can hear us. It's natural to want someone close to share your dreams with. Don't let your dreams be too wild, too free, too big, or too original is what we discover when we don't get support from our families. Your dreams will never be good enough for some, yet your dreams can be too much for others. There may always be someone who attempts to keep you in the same box they live in! People like what's familiar to them, and sometimes, when you step outside of the norm, your family is first to crucify your dreams! Beware! This aspect of human nature is why you can't rely on your family exclusively as your *only* form of support.

Stop telling your family members every business idea unless they are your business partners. I had to learn how to keep some things to myself and share my business ideas with those who could give me objective business advice. Do not let your family stunt your growth with their judgment. Your family may mean well, and yet they need to stay out of your business decisions. Unless you are using their money to fund your business and they are 51% owners. There is nothing wrong with leaning on supportive family for emotional support, yet for the sake of sanity, keep your family and your business 99.9% separate, unless it's a family business. Everyone will be happy!

And Organizations Fail You

Initially, when I conducted my business research, my goal was to locate 20 African American female business owners who met two criteria. First, the women had maintained businesses for at least five years. Second, they were members of the National Association of Women Business Owners (NAWBO). However, locating 20 participants that met the study's specific criteria was nearly impossible. Part of the difficulty arose because I found it challenging to get a commitment from the business owners. Yet to my surprise, most of my challenges came from formal business organizations designed to help women.

I experienced a strong lack of participation from managers of the NAWBO organization. I contacted 30 NAWBO managers via phone and email to distribute information about the study to their members. However, only two out of the 30 NAWBO managers distributed information to their members. The 28 non-responsive NAWBO managers were contacted a second time by email and phone. None of the other 28 NAWBO managers responded to my email or phone requests. The two managers who agreed to distribute information about the survey to their members did not have many African American female business owners who met the study's criteria.

Neither did the NAWBO organizations located in cities with high African American populations have many African American female members. Some NAWBO chapters did not have any African American members. Business organizations (that catered to the development of female business owners, other than the NAWBO), were briefly considered. I dismissed contacting those smaller organizations because of the lack of members who met the criteria. It was a frustrating experience, to say the least. Ironically, the women I researched also didn't have pleasant experiences with formal business organizations that offer to help women business owners.

Memberships within formal women business organizations were not listed as necessarily helpful to the African American female entrepreneur. Notably, one participant stated that she did not feel "welcome or accepted" within some networks geared toward women entrepreneurs. We don't feel welcomed by formal organizations. This lack of acceptance has to change. There are however, networks of support that welcome you with open doors.

Not every formal organization is the same. Where you don't see networks of support, we have to get resourceful and create them. The consensus was that African American female entrepreneurs did not necessarily have the same types of support systems as those of White female business owners. Therefore, African American female entrepreneurs had to get creative in establishing their own networks of support, unique and specific to their needs. Identified support needs included the need for self-support, surrounding oneself with positive people, and using religious faith as a tool to feel spiritually supported by a higher power.

African American women tend to get their business support from non-formal faith-based organizations like churches. I am here to tell you that the church *aint* enough. A church is great in that it can help you strengthen your faith and feel less stressed emotionally. In reality, when it comes to providing business support, the church of 2020 is inadequate. Once upon a time, African American churches played a substantial role in providing help to African American business owners. Historically, churches were safe havens for African Americans. They gave business owners tools and support, at a time when there weren't many other options for African American business owners wanting to organize. It's 2020 now; churches operate like the businesses they are. The church's mission is to grow its business, not your business. Most churches are nonprofits and non-formal organizations. They need you and the government to pour resources into their business. African American women business owners need professional business support from organizations that support African American women's growth *and* can *see* them.

We need to create meeting places where we feel like we can let both our hair and guards down. We need safe havens where we can be seen and connect to other successful women. These women can teach us how to be successful. What we currently have available is simply not fucking enough. Why isn't it enough? It's not enough because the research shows we lack support from formal and informal organizations. African American women feel ignored! African American women feel unseen and unheard. The irony is that African American women are starting businesses faster than any other group; that's one reason to pay attention to what they are doing. An African American woman is also more likely not to experience business success. That means she needs help even though she is a go-getter! She needs support.

There are issues in business that are specific to African American women and their experience in being an entrepreneur. No one talks about them because they don't know about it. People don't know the depth of these issues because of our lack of exploring African American women business owners' experiences. We see African American women starting businesses, and for some reason, that's good enough. But it's not good enough if those businesses fail or if she does not see the same level of success (especially financial success) as her peers. We need to start working with organizations that see and hear us. And stop supporting those organizations that don't want to include us at the main table. We don't need organizations that victimize or pity us. We do need organizations that hear our experience.

We need organizations that create unique ways to help us advance and become better business owners. For every area where such an organization does not exist, we need to create it. There is a saying that if you don't like something, then change it. The time is now for us to create communities of support where there are shared resources. We need access to the main table, where experts from all varieties are seated, specifically to help us advance.

Fuck with Those That Fuck with You

It's time to explore frontiers that you wouldn't normally explore and seek out those who want to connect with you. It's time for the African American woman to come out of hiding and isolation. There is an entire world that is ready to embrace you! There are seven continents for you to build on. The only limitation is the one you set for yourself. It's a myth that the world does not like African American women. Actually, it's an outright lie. The moment you step out of your shell, someone will welcome you, trust me! There are almost eight billion people on this planet. I guarantee you have a soul tribe out there.

A soul tribe is a group of people that you resonate with; they may or may not be within your ethnic group. We keep ourselves lonely when we refuse to reach out because of fear of rejection. And I understand why. Yet if we continue to allow the sins of a few to paint a narrative for our future, we will never build the relationships with others that we need to build. We fear we are going to be rejected because of our experiences. We allow painful experiences to taint our view of all people. We don't give people a chance, yet sometimes when we do, we get hurt! That's the risk we all take, goddess. Don't let a few painful experiences keep you in your shell. Don't let rumors of people not liking African American women keep you from making friends from all backgrounds.

We have to learn to love ourselves and each other. Before you can do that effectively, you must self-heal. The more you love and accept yourself, the more you will attract those that love and accept you. The more you step out, travel, and see the world, the more you will see that not every country is obsessed with racism like America. Moreover, the more you travel within the United States, the more you will notice that people (in general) are not fixated on race like you thought. You were taught a lie. Now it's time to let the lie go. Step out and see for yourself. You are bound to run into assholes and angels of all kinds. Your color only matters as much as you focus on it. When I see people, I see myself. And I get treated like I treat others 99 percent of the time. If you start your relationships with your guards up, you may manifest a reason to have your guards up. Concisely, if you are lonely in business, realize that you don't have to be. There are creative solutions to developing professional networks, which we will explore in the next section.

Creating Sister Support

Just as it is essential to branch out and connect to likeminded people from all ethnicities for the purpose of growing your business and fostering diversity, it's especially important to learn how to work with other African American women. It's time to end the cultural stigma that suggests that African American people can't do business with other African American people and that women don't get along. It is a myth that African American women business owners don't support one another. On the contrary, your sisters that look like you can also support you. They can assist you just as well as any ethnicity. If someone is qualified to help you grow, they can help you grow because they have the tools to do it. The fact that they may be African American does not mean they (automatically) can't help you, and it doesn't mean they (automatically) can help you either. If you have trust issues with African American women, you won't work with them. You won't give her a chance to see what she can do for you or how you may work together. Some successful African American women have resources that can help you in your business. Don't you have skills that you can share? That means other people do, too. Skills didn't stop and start with you.

You sabotage yourself by refusing to work with other women business owners. You lose your opportunity to connect on a personal level with someone who looks like you. It's within these types of groups that African American women may feel the psychological and emotional support needed to create a successful business. One of the reasons African American women avoid professional organizations is because they feel excluded. The research suggests that there is an underrepresentation of African American women within organizations designed to help women business owners. Sometimes you don't want to get on a blow horn to be heard and force people to accept you. You don't have to either. There is a relief that comes with being heard. Sometimes you need someone to talk to, and you don't have to explain shit—someone who can relate directly to you so that you feel heard and understood. Befriend a professional, relatable qualified African American woman. She's not a unicorn if you expand where you are looking. The myth of women always fighting and competing with each other is just that, a myth. Women do know how to work together; in fact, that is what we *do* naturally. Women work together and are willing to work together more so than men, who are often more competitive with each other. A woman will give you information, write it down, and tell you how she acquired her millions.

The media floods us with negative images of angry African American women, behaving badly towards each other. It's easy to fall into the trap of thinking that women are nasty, will smile in your face and stab you in your back. Yet we know that's logically not true. There are trust issues that we need to go beyond; some of these trust issues come from our cultural history of learning to distrust one another. Distrust is reiterated in television and media. It is a mental disorder when you *automatically* don't trust and misjudge someone because they look like you. It means you have an issue with yourself. Everyone has the potential to help you, and everyone has the potential to destroy your trust. The possibility is always fucking 50/50, no matter what their appearance. You cut potentially good people out of your life with your bias of refusing to work with and network with African American women. At the end of the day, you want to open yourself up to work with everyone whom you resonate with and who have something to teach you, African American women (definitely) included.

Find Your Soul Tribe in a Mastermind Group

Once you expand your horizons and open yourself to working with qualified networks of support, you will find that there are several ways to go about building networks. One way of expanding your network is through attending and participating in Masterminds. Masterminds are groups of people who come together to brainstorm, educate, and create accountability. Masterminds are great ways to connect with experts within your industry within a group setting, to sharpen your business and personal skills. Masterminds can help you develop your business because it creates accountability amongst members. Mastermind groups can help you create and reach your goals. Often Masterminds have facilitators that start and run Mastermind groups.

Group facilitators often lead deep-dive discussions and help members to be successful in their business by providing tools to help them advance. I've facilitated and attended Masterminds. As a guest, Masterminds allow you to improve and deepen your knowledge base; you become privy to information that ideally cuts your business success learning curve. As a Mastermind facilitator, Masterminds are a fantastic way to develop your tribe and extend your business reach.

Masterminds bring industry leaders together to provide an atmosphere of camaraderie. Masterminds often meet monthly and have a group agenda. The agenda within Mastermind meetings may focus on expanding the knowledge base for group members as a collective. For example, how to effectively use messenger bots to drive sales through Instant Messenger. Or the agenda may focus on providing resolutions for your specific issue. For example, reviewing your website content to make sure it is compliant, assuming you have a compliance expert in your Mastermind. Masterminds help you grow because a good Mastermind group will give you constructive criticism from your peers and offer you new ideas. The group can help you develop your thoughts using group brainpower. It is priceless to tap into the knowledge base of someone else, and Masterminds allow you to do just that. One of the keys to success is to surround yourself with people who are smarter than you. Masterminds put you in a position of sitting with wise counsel, and the attention you receive is targeted, compared to getting lost in large organizations.

Smaller groups make it easier to be heard and seen. With Masterminds, you can work efficiently with a smaller group. You get things done because you can't hide amongst your peers. It's harder to get lost in the shuffle, and it creates a keen sense of accountability. Finally, Masterminds help you build your confidence by allowing you to help others with your knowledge, skill, or expertise. You gain confidence by showing your peers what you've learned. Joining a Mastermind is the perfect addition to joining formal organizations. It's a productive place to build your support network.

The Coaching, Consulting, and Mentorship Models

Coaching, consulting, and mentorship are excellent ways to create a network of support. I like all of these options, because similar to Masterminds, you often have access to a smaller group, and individualized attention. Successful people have networks of support in every area of their lives. The bonus with coaching, consulting, and mentorship is that you typically have the option of one-on-one assistance. Essentially all of the models overlap in the various areas of service they provide, as you will see below. However, there are differences between each paradigm.

Rather than see each model as completely separate, I prefer to look at coaching, consulting, and mentoring as three offerings that provide one universal solution to their clients…*to give you the extra human support you need from someone outside of yourself, with an expert who can add to your success.*

All three models provide the bird's-eye view necessary for success. Pulling in an expert from the outside can give you a greater perspective. How each model goes about doing that depends on the model. Each model can blend into the other, *and* all three models can stand alone as a unique offering. For visualization, consider the upside-down triangle in the example below. Each model lies within the triangle. Coaching occurs in the widest part of the triangle; mentorship rests in the triangle's middle, and consulting lies within the narrowest part of the triangle. The triangle narrows as each service becomes more specific in its offering to the client. The triangle can be viewed from the bottom up, top-down, or from the middle out. Where you start or engage within the triangle will be based on you as a business owner, and *exactly* what type of support you need. You may also find that you benefit from engaging in all three models during your business career, again depending on your needs.

Coaches. You want to hire a coach when you need to be cheered on and improve your performance. They help you improve your act within a given area. You can hire them to help advance a specific business area and to provide general information, such as increasing sales. Coaches can encourage you to reach your goals. Hire a coach when you know what you're doing, yet you need to tighten up and be pushed. Because a coach specializes in human behavior, it does not matter what industry your business is in; they are there to make you perform better.

Hire a coach when you need to develop skills. Coaches can help you brainstorm. They don't advise their clients like mentors and consultants; instead, coaches help clients produce their own solutions. Coaches place the responsibility on the client to complete their tasks. It's up to the client to do the work to get the results they want. When you think of the purpose and function of a coach, picture the energy of your favorite sports coach. This is the person who can pick up your spirits when you're in the middle of losing.

Coaches look at how you perform, and they are expecting you to do specific plays to win. Coaches can help you identify your blind spots so that you could avoid potential disaster. They share with you ways you can improve your abilities. Coaches can help you see your strengths and help you aim for higher outcomes. Coaches sharpen you. They make you quicker by emphasizing the improvement of your overall routine. They are wonderful people to add to your network. Mentoring can take you deeper because mentors typically have more experience.

Mentors. A mentor is a teacher. And a teacher is only a teacher after they have learned something. Mentors teach you based on the knowledge that they have acquired. The levels of expertise may vary between you and your mentor. A mentor may even be willing to work for free. They are an individual that has accomplished something they set out to do, and now, they want to help you. When you look for a mentor, you are looking for someone who has more experience than you do *and* someone who can enhance your professional growth. The mentor is the person who passes information, skills, and wisdom down to the mentee. Ideally, when the mentee applies the knowledge, they become successful. The mentor is there to share what they've discovered. A coach is not necessarily a subject matter expert. A mentor is intelligent because of knowledge, and they share based on what has worked for them in the past.

The mentor's focus is directly on the individual's development; the coach's mindset is on task completion. The mentor focuses on whom the client needs to *become* to be successful compared to coaches that focus on *what* a client needs *to do*. Mentors advise on what you need to do differently *and* what works for the business. Mentors have a strategy to give you based on their own playbook. They are solid members to add to your team. A good mentor will empower you with their words by motivating you to be accountable. They can help you create a strategy to achieve your specific business goal. A mentor will enhance your professionalism. A coach will improve your behavior. And they can both contribute to your knowledge and growth. A consultant can take you deeper than both a coach and a mentor because of their blend of *specific industry* knowledge and expertise.

Consultants. Consultants are some of the best people to add to your team. They are experts within a specific field. And they can offer professional or technical advice through tutoring, instructing, or training. Consultants are helpful when you need specific assistance within an industry. For example, if you wanted to start a CBD company, you wouldn't seek out a coach for general information. You would hire a consultant because they have *experience* and *knowledge* within your *specific* industry. They have knowledge based upon their lived experienced, not only the experience of others. Good consultants introduce you to their Black book. Their Black book consists of other professionals within the field who have a specific area of expertise. Like merchant account processors for CBD companies, for example. Consultants can cut your learning curve and save you time and money.

They can do this because they have already made some of the mistakes you made 100 times over. Therefore, they are genuinely giving you information based on where they have been. Unlike coaching, where the answers come from the client, mentors and consultants provide solutions to clients. Both resources are a perfect option for clients that desire direct professional advice. Consultants are not guessing; they give information based on experience. They know how to succeed and have a successful working relationship with others; consultants have a record of accomplishments. When you need to discover the who, what, where, when, why, and how within your field, it's time to hire a consultant. When you need access to resources that can help you move forward, it's time to hire a consultant. Where coaches may offer action plans based on general information and mentors offer advice from their knowledge, consultants offer expert guidance to a precise group of people within a specific industry. Consultants are considered authorities within their field because of the work they've done. They are much more specific than coaches who can be generalists in their services. Mentors and consultants can offer you advice. Yet the guidance from mentors will typically be wide-ranging and not necessarily based on definite industry knowledge. Consultants are great when you need specific tools and information to help you succeed.

Coaches, mentors, and consultants can each help you and your business develop. When you hire any of these professionals, you may see improvements within your behavior and business. You may even find that you holistically improve, spiritually, mentally, and physically. Adding professionals to your network will ensure you are not the smartest person in the room. Surrounding yourself with people who can help you reach your goals is better than surrounding yourself with people who have not reached their goals yet. Professionals show you how to get from A-to-Z. Professionals can help you by lending their expertise within their areas of specialization. Professionals deserve a seat at your executive table. These are the people you want to bounce your business questions off and get their opinion of your business strategy.

Professionals have "qualified opinions." And they are qualified because they have the knowledge and/or know-how, based on field knowledge and working with others. You may have a professional in every area of your life, pushing you towards expansion. Their opinions are beyond what they feel, think, or believe. Their opinions are based on facts. You must always use discernment when listening to any opinion. Be especially careful when offered advice from a nonprofessional without experience. You would not ask a person who knows nothing about architecture to help you draw a blueprint for a house. Ask people who know what they are talking about questions only they can answer. You have to consider the source where you get your information and realize that you can't ask everyone the same question. If you want to expand your network and grow, start by surrounding yourself with people who can answer all your damn questions and share resources that you did not know existed.

Network Through Social Media

There are many ways to network and cultivate your professional support base. As mentioned previously, you can gain momentum by networking within formal organizations, and by receiving one-on-one support from specialists. Yet there is another way to grow your support network and meet likeminded people. That way is through utilizing social media.

Facebook. Pretty much the whole world appears as if it's on Facebook. As of December 2019, Facebook estimated there were over 2.8 billion people who used Facebook regularly. There are eight billion people on the planet. Facebook can be used productively and can manufacture positive results. There are over 16 million local business pages on Facebook. It's normal to conduct business on Facebook. You can use Facebook as a tool for marketing, targeting your audience, and analyzing advertising results. You can even make sales on Facebook using messenger bots! Yet, did you know that Facebook is a great platform to connect to like-minded people? I'm not talking about connecting to the friends on your personal page, that's what you do for fun unless your friends are all professionals. I am speaking of connecting through Facebook groups.

There are over 400 million people on active Facebook groups, and Facebook allows you to join up to 6,000 groups. Facebook groups are people who share the same interest and meet on Facebook within private or public forums. You may join a Facebook group that focuses on branding, building, or scaling your CBD business, like the group, CBD Business Success. Facebook groups help to connect you with people around the world within a shared community. Industry professionals lead some groups. The key is to do your research by verifying the source and the validity of the offered information. Facebook groups are typically useful for asking broad questions and/or reaching out to other business owners for support. I like groups because you don't feel alone when you are part of a group. Suddenly you step, "Into the light Carolynn..." and you surround yourself with a feeling of encouragement[61]. Group support is especially helpful if you are feeling hopeless, and you need a "pick me up." Groups can help lighten your mood, and perhaps you will learn added information. You can immediately start connecting with others—today! Another bonus is that often these groups are free. Free groups can provide a way to extend your network. With 400 million people participating in Facebook groups, you would be remiss not to join one.

LinkedIn: I hope to god that you are on LinkedIn if you are a business owner looking to grow your professional network. Why? Because LinkedIn is like Facebook in that you have access to people from around the globe. LinkedIn has 630 million members. I think of LinkedIn as the grown-up Facebook. People who join LinkedIn are generally doing so to connect to other professional people. They are not on LinkedIn to play games and make posts about mindless things that no one cares about. LinkedIn can help you build brand awareness, build your creditability, and create engaging posts. LinkedIn can help you build your professional audience. This social media platform is an excellent way to form your email list by connecting to people who are within your industry. LinkedIn is also wonderful because it is Cannabis and CBD business-friendly, more so than Facebook. It is easy to find people within your expertise throughout the world. LinkedIn allows you to attract people to you. These are people who may be interested in networking opportunities. You attract people by highlighting your offerings within your LinkedIn profile. The more complete your profile, the more other professionals will take you seriously and make a connection. LinkedIn provides another free way to exchange emails, reach out, and find people you can add to your network.

Instagram: As of 2019, there were one billion users on Instagram. This scope makes Instagram the most engaged social network after Facebook. People are constantly on their phones in 2020, and they like to connect on social media. You can take advantage of that. Instagram helps you to network by getting your business name in the spotlight. People will want to follow to see what you are up to; you can also follow others to build your network. You draw people by creating engaging, attractive posts. Instagram does a magnificent job of letting you reach out to your network. One way of doing this is by creating a video chat and responding to another's chat. There are also Instagram groups you can join that share the same industry. I like Instagram because it feels like a support network. You support another business by following them.

You can also communicate with people in a casual yet professional manner through Instagram's Direct Messenger. Instagram lets people know you are serious about connecting when you take advantage of all the tools available, like its group chat feature. Instagram lets you use hashtags (#) to get more engagements. You are allowed up to 30 hashtags in a single post. These hashtags help you gain new followers, helps people find you on Instagram and encourages post engagement. Instagram is a fun way to play on the internet productively while building your support group.

Meetup: Why rely on someone else to find like-minds? Meetup is considered a social media site, although you do not have followers like on Instagram or other direct online connections. This platform offers a profound way to make friends and add to your support system and network. Meetup is literally meant for people who want to meet-up—in person or online.

If you want to meet and connect through mutual interests, then Meetup is for you. Meetup allows members to self-organize, plus it's easy to use. What I love about Meetup is the variety of groups that you can connect with, like joining a travel group or exploring a foreign language with a group that meets at a local restaurant. Joining these groups can add to your personal, professional, and business growth. You get to cultivate, nurture, and/or improve what matters to you with others who want to do the same.

Meetup can get you out of entrepreneur isolation and foster connections with other business owners. Meetup is great for networking because people attend with a mission to connect. There is no need for an ice breaker. It's less awkward than joining a group where people have to be coaxed into participating. In a meetup, the expectation is that everyone will participate when you "meetup," otherwise you defeat the purpose of the encounter. Adding a Meetup group to your support network tool kit can open the door to long-lasting relationships. To date, there are 225K Meetup groups in 180 countries. There are over 35 million Meetup users. All Meetup groups have different topics, and each group has its own size and rules. Some groups are free. Some groups charge a small fee, and donations fund other groups. Most Meetup events are scheduled weekly or monthly at local sites or online. Meetup is a casual, steady way to find other business owners, share your hobby, and/or network with other professionals.

There are many traditional and nontraditional ways to expand your network. The information provided in this section offer solutions to African American women networkers. From using formal organizations to using social media as a means of support. The more support you feel as a business owner, the better your confidence and the stronger you will feel. When you have tools, there is nothing that will be able to keep you from reaching your goals. The best thing about building a cushion of support is that you can create and use many of these ideas simultaneously.

I recommend that you set up a layered system of support. You want to create a hedge of successful people around you and position yourself in the center of this system. If you add prosperous people in your life, people who can teach you, then you will set your business up for amazing success.

Part III: My Story—Messes Become Messages

Throughout my life, I have been surrounded by people that expected more out of me. They expected me to live my best life. Of course, there were also some negative people around me that I could not control while growing up, but I chose to focus on the beings that supported my growth. Even those people who were negative added to my success. I used negative situations to push me forward. Everyone has a story and a past; we can choose to allow our negative experiences or challenges growing-up to hold us back or set us free. We've all had what we would consider unpleasant experiences growing up, that we must heal from if we want to experience true success.

It was common to hear rumors that I would be the first one to get pregnant simply because I began developing curves early. I grew up hearing things like, "Watch out," and "fast" about my frame—comments like those made me feel awful within my own skin. And unbeknownst to anyone, I was being molested regularly from when I was five years old until I was 15 years old. I was a virgin who survived 10 years of sexual abuse. I survived the abuse because I never let it define me. I refused to be a victim and I fought to keep my virginity.

I developed enough strength to say *No*. Learning how to say *No*, will save your life goddess. I didn't have my biological father present; I had to heal from rejection and abandonment. To heal myself and stand in my own power, I learned how to allow my emotions flow. This is important to your success—allowing yourself to feel your emotions. We can choose to believe the lies we heard growing up, or we can declare our own truths. We can allow past experiences to affect our success, and we can create mental blockages that we cannot seem to get past or heal from. Or we can choose the path of forgiveness in all things and move forward. Ultimately, if you choose the latter, this may positively affect your relationship with others and your relationship with yourself.

Occasionally having a rough time growing up is what motivates you to succeed as an adult. People did not always treat me well, and like most kids, I experienced bullying growing up. I did not develop more confidence until the 8th grade after I read, *I Know Why the Caged Bird Sings* by Maya Angelou. For some reason, that book gave me the extra oomph that I needed to step into my authentic, weird, and unique self. Maybe it was the same for you. Perhaps you recently decided to wear your hair in a natural style, and that choice is helping you explore your unique beauty and self. When I was growing up, it had not been decided if the brown girl was in or out. This was in the 80s, when melanin was not "popping" in the mainstream, like it is now. You had to have self-esteem for real in the 80s! Finding your identity, embracing the beauty that you are inside and out, and recognizing the gifts you have helps you to build your self-esteem and attract more success in your life. Self-esteem has been paramount for me. There is no way I could be a successful entrepreneur without self-esteem. Self-esteem helps you to have faith in yourself and a higher Self.

Unhealed past trauma during our formative years can affect how we respond to life. Instead of losing control or forfeiting my success, I chose to use the doubts of others to propel me forward. For every negative situation I encountered growing up, I experienced an army of angels in disguise. These people pushed me to move forward like my dance instructors and college professors who expected more out of me. And of course, my parents who continue to propel me forward with their support. I am lucky that my mother remarried later in life to a man whom I consider to be my dad. Overall, I grew up with people expecting more out of me. I learned to expect more out of myself.

Victory didn't happen for me right away as an entrepreneur. My passion for success was ignited long before I became a business owner. And I am grateful because having a mindset rooted in success has made it easier to get into business and eventually see success. If it weren't for my expectation of (eventual) victory, I would've quit a long time ago. Yet this is my passion. Working for yourself may indeed be the secret to happiness. Whatever mess you experienced in the past can indeed become your message.

My Entrepreneur Spirit

I've always been into doing my own thing. It's even better when you can make money and help people-while doing your own thing. That is the spirit of being an entrepreneur for me. That's the freedom that attracted me. Working for yourself equals freedom and the ability to make money using your creative gifts while providing a product or service that's honorable. I grew up wanting to work for myself. I grew up wanting to use my gifts to produce wealth. I was naturally gifted with abilities; we all are. Maybe you have forgotten?

Remember when you were a kid, and there were certain things you could do naturally or were drawn to do, and others struggled? Talents and hobbies that you participated in? Remember the things you did just for fun? Maybe you were into sports and naturally athletic? Perhaps you have managed to maintain that philosophy well into your adult years? Maybe, now as an adult, you run a health supplement company because the business aligns with your natural passion for things health related.

Those things you find easy to do, where others may struggle, are hidden talents that you may sell. People will pay you for your skills. People will reward you for your knowledge. As a little girl, I wanted to be a professional singer. That was my first career choice. I knew at five years old that when I became an adult, I wanted to do a job that I loved, and that didn't feel like work.

I was serious about reaching my goals. I can remember practicing my songs, doing mock interviews with talk show hosts about my success, and practicing writing my autograph for imagined fans. Society did not see my dream of becoming a professional singer realistic. So, like many children who want to make their parents happy and get a reliable *job* when they grow up, I put my dream of being a singer on hold. Eventually, I joined the workforce at the age of 14. But I was not happy about it. I accepted life as this place where you work hard for someone else. I was never completely satisfied *because* I was working for someone else. I quickly realized growing up that the jobs I enjoyed the most were the jobs where I was allowed to be creative and have input in decision making. As a preteen, I could see the power and importance of having a leadership role as a worker. I enjoyed babysitting growing up because babysitting taught me how to manage my time and clients. I even worked as a Mary Kay consultant at 18 years old.

The entrepreneurial spirit arose strongly in me in 2003, when I was working in the medical records section at the VA Hospital. I took a pay cut to work in Medical Records. I left the police department so that I could finish my master's degree program. In other words, I took a demotion to promote myself. Working in Medical Records gave me the timeout that I needed to try different things with my life and see what I really wanted to do.

I thought that, maybe, I would go into law school after I got my master's degree. I took the LSAT and only applied to one school; that dream did not pan out. Then I thought maybe I would go into the FBI and eventually become an agent. I applied for a position at the FBI and went through the entire hiring process, and that did not manifest either. After experiencing two dream career disappointments, I can remember sitting at my work computer in the file room, and I had an epiphany.

Maybe it was meant for me to create my dream job? Maybe my path was one of an entrepreneur. Perhaps my life path was not about making someone else rich? Perhaps my life work would come from doing something I enjoyed, like helping people and making money at the same time. And so, it happened, I remember thinking about my life and what I wanted to do with myself beyond attending school and working for the government. I asked myself what I really wanted. That afternoon in the file room, I created an elaborate entrepreneur plan. I remember feeling electricity run through me as I visualized working for myself. I imagined the possibilities. I pictured the services I would offer.

My very first business idea was to open an elaborate spa. I was nowhere near having the resources to create that specific plan in 2003. Nonetheless, I could see that I really wanted to work for myself because it was easy for me to create a service. Writing out the vision of having my own company in that lonely forgotten file room was empowering. I knew that even if I didn't become an entrepreneur who owned a spa, that I was going to work for myself eventually—because it was meant for me to do so.

Nothing, not even the good and meaningful careers that I had throughout my 20s and 30s were enough, for me. Something was always missing. I had a desire to control and create my own shit, and I discovered what was missing while working literally in the basement of the VA hospital. My life path didn't take me into business right away. Oh no. Of course, I continued to work for the VA, get promoted, and learn more. My passion for success caused me to pick up additional skills, education, and more resources while working for others. Until I created my own business, I treated every job I had like I was the CEO. This perspective caused me to give my all in every position I worked and made me phenomenally successful in every role that I held. I was able to pick-up the pertinent skills that I use today as a business owner. Skills that I have discussed throughout this book.

My Passion for Women

I love all women, and I hope that you feel my love through the words I chose in this book. I've always had a powerful desire to help women, especially overlooked melanated women. Because of this desire to reach and teach women, in 2013, I gave birth to a company called Women's Circle International (WCI). I remember like it was yesterday, I was sitting in my car, and I was again contemplating what I wanted to do with my life. Then suddenly, I felt the words *help women* flash across my face. Then I was told by my intuition that I was to author a book and have a conference. I immediately got to work on the idea, and it was a huge undertaking. I decided to focus on the conference aspect of Women's Circle International.

Six months after sitting in my car with just an idea, I launched my first holistic health conference for women in downtown Milwaukee. I had over 30 holistic health industry vendors and close to one hundred paid guests. The event included a holistic health swag bag, lunch, access to several holistic health speakers, access to a fashion show, a silent auction, and out-of-state keynote speakers. It attracted guests from out-of-state, and this was my first time doing an event of such magnitude. I even had an Art Gallery afterparty for my VIP guests.

I designed my first company for women around the idea of conducting holistic health workshops around the topics of mental, physical, and emotional healing. I wanted to create a network of support for women to learn how to live holistically and connect with other women internationally while doing so. I wanted to teach women how to heal themselves by offering workshops, conferences, and gatherings to share resources on holistic living. So, I did just that.

I held conferences and events within the Milwaukee area. I branched out, and for the first time as an entrepreneur, I affected change internationally by participating in a charity event in Ghana, West Africa. I had not been in business for seven months, and I was already living up to my title by helping women on an international level. My early contribution was small. I had no profits to show, and yet I felt like I had accomplished a part of my vision— helping women.

WCI was the first company that I created where I narrowed my key audience to women. Knowing whom I was talking to made it much easier to market. I knew my audience, so I knew where to advertise. There were certain magazines that my target read, and that is how I used my extremely limited marketing and advertising budget. I also opted for radio interviews on stations that would give me a chance to talk about the event. And of course, like any grassroots marketing, I used friend- and family-labor to spread the word. It worked! I reached people from across the states and flew guests in from California to Wisconsin. Me—this little girl from Wisconsin, who had just decided months ago to leave her secure government job and start a company. I built a website six months before launching my first conference. Another critical point, I quickly built traffic because blogging was popular.

By 2013, I learned a thing or two about search engine optimization (SEO) from getting my toes wet with my first e-commerce store. To help my SEO for my website, I created blogs; each blog addressed holistic health topics. Then I created my first Facebook account for business and posted my information there. The very reason I created a Facebook account was for business because Facebook was a growing supergiant for business connections. In the early Facebook days, my limited knowledge of how to use it and its less feature-rich software affected my outreach efforts. Nevertheless, I was able to build a presence on Facebook, which helped bring legitimacy to my brand. Looking back on my first business concepts, I realize I suffered from trying to balance too many tasks while running Women's Circle International.

I eventually got the universal message and courage to part ways with all my jobs and distractions and work exclusively for myself in 2016. Almost 10 years into my entrepreneurial journey, which I talk about throughout this book. Although I was not working for the government (in my WCI days), I was still juggling multiple jobs and projects like a madwoman. I also suffered from not offering the right services to sustain my business model and put capital back into my business. I did have a membership subscription model, but in 2013, however, I didn't know enough about marketing my paid group through Facebook. Plus, Facebook was the place people wanted to socialize. If you wanted to pull people from a Facebook group to a paid forum, you had to have a compelling offer. To put it differently, I had to have an offer that was captivating enough to secure lots of members.

Long after I launched Women's' Circle, I continued to work on my offerings. I went back and forth with the idea of writing a book for women. Long after my first successful women's conference, I continued to brainstorm and develop other products and services that would help women. In 2015 I expanded beyond WCI, and I found my roots within the cannabis industry. I am proud to say that I still help women heal themselves holistically. Now

I have added cannabis to help assist that process. Cannabis has helped me explore my passion for helping women heal holistically, which is what I ultimately set out to do with other businesses. I built cannabis into my business product and service offering. I've always been passionate about women in general and our issues. Why not create a business you are passionate about?

Create a Business You Enjoy

It's time to expect more out of your life situation and create a business you enjoy. Step out of someone else's dream and live your own reality! In this book, I've given you the history of African American Business, Five Keys to Create A Successful Business, and I've shared my personal experiences. It's time for you to let this information sit with you, study, and apply it. You can bring about the transformation you would like to see within the world by using your gifts and abilities. You can make money working your passion. I am a living witness. We are no different from one another, goddess. If you have made it to the end of this book and read every chapter, I am especially talking to you!

Not everyone makes it to the end of the book! Reaching this point shows that you are dedicated to your success. You may already have a business, and yet you don't feel fulfilled because you know you are playing it small. You might be holding yourself and your business back out of fear and self-sabotaging your destiny. You want to grow—yet you've been intimidated. Maybe you've let the jealously of others hinder your success, and you've been listening to naysayers. I am here to sound the alarm and reawaken your soul wisdom. Despite any negative energy that may come against you, Melanated Star Seed, you were born to be successful. You have the right to live your vision, and now you have the tools! You have the right to expect fucking more! It is your birthright, along with everyone else! Yes! You can absolutely build a successful business. Study and apply the Five Keys of Business Success outlined in this book and create the business you enjoy today!

Hello Goddess!

Connect to your soul business tribe beyond this book!

Keep up with me at drbeethomas.com.

Take your learning deeper with our Expect More course.

Turn your study into action within your business.

Discover which actionable steps you need to take next.

Use the code EXPECTMORE for 25% off the course.

See you soon!

Xoxo Dr. Bee

Endnotes

1 American Express, "State of Women Owned Business Report," (Ventureneer, 2018).

2 National Women's Business Council "Advancing Women Entrepreneurs. Growing America's Economy," (2019), http://www.nwbc.gov.

3 Singh, R., Knox, E., Crump, E. S. Opportunity recognition differences between Black and White nascent entrepreneurs: A test of the Bhave's model. *Journal of Developmental Entrepreneurship*, 19, (2008): 174-196.

4 Bates, T. and Lofstrom, M., "African American's Pursuit of Self Employment," (IZA Discussion Paper No. 3156), (Bonn, Germany: Institute for the Study of Labor, 2007, November), http://ftp.iza.org/dp3156.pdf.

5 Smith-Hunter, A. and Kapp, J., "Minority Women Entrepreneurs and the Impediments They Face in the Engineering, Mining, and Construction Fields," *The Journal of Applied Business and Economics* 10, no. 2 (2009): 36-49.

6 Stevens, T., "Victims and Victors: Facing the Challenges of Changing Times," *Journal of Economics and Economic Education Research* 11, no. 3 (2010): 87-105.

7 Puryear, A. N., Rogoff, E., Lee, M., Heck, R. K., Grossman, E. B., Haynes, G. W., and Onochie, J., "Sampling Minority Business Owners and Their Families: The Understudied Entrepreneurial Experience," *Journal of Small Business Management* 46, no. 3 (2008): 422-455.

8 Devnew, L. E., "Enactment: A Powerful Concept in a Changing World," Paper presented at the meeting of the *Management 711: Strategic opportunities in an Internet-based global economy*, (2008).

9 Hormat, R., "The Future of America's Financial Dominance," *The International Economy* 22, no. 4 (2008): 40-87.

10   Veira, X., "A Comparison Between Female and Male Entrepreneurs in the Perspective of Gender Equality and Empowerment of Women, the Third Goal on the List of Millennium Development Goals. *Global Watch* 3, no. 1 (2008): 95-99.

11   U.S. Small Business Administration, "Research and Statistics," (2007), http://www.sba.gov.

12   U.S. Small Business Administration, "Small Business Profile," (2018), www.sba.gov.

13   Spector, R. *The Mom & Pop Store: How the Unsung Heroes of the American Economy are Surviving and Thriving.* Walker & Company, (2009).

14   Garrett-Scott, S., "A Historiography of African American Business," *Business and Economic History On-Line* 7, (2009), http://www.thebhc. org/ publications/BEHonline/2009/garrett-scott.pdf.

15   Fairlie, R. W. and Robb, A. M., "Families, Human Capital, and Small Business: Evidence From the Characteristics of Business Owners Survey," *Industrial and Labor Relations Review* 60, no. 2 (2007a): 225-245.

16   Lussier, R. N. and Halabi, C. E., "A Three-Country Comparison of the Business Success Versus Failure Prediction Model," *Journal of Small Business Management* 48, (2010): 360-377.

17   Sullivan, T. A. and McCracken, S. D., "Black Entrepreneurs: Patterns and Rates of Return to Self-Employment," *National Journal of Sociology* 2, no. 2 (1988): 165-185.

18   Edelman, L. F., Brush, C. G., Manolova, T. S., and Greene, P. G., "Start-Up Motivations and Growth Intentions of Minority Nascent Entrepreneurs," *Journal of Small Business Management* 48, no. 2 (2010): 174-196.

19   Sullivan, T. A., & McCracken, S. D. (1988). Black Entrepreneurs: Patterns and Rates of Return to Self-Employment. *National Journal of Sociology*, 2(2), 165-185.

20   Singh, R., Knox, E., Crump, E. S. Opportunity Recognition Differences Between Black and White Nascent Entrepreneurs: A Test of the Bhave's Model. *Journal of Developmental Entrepreneurship*, 19, (2008): 174-196.

21 Gold, S. J., "Immigrant Entrepreneurs' Relations With Customers in the Early 20th Century US," Paper presented at the American Sociological Association Annual Meeting, Boston, MA. (2008), http://www.allacademic.com/meta/ p238764 index.htm.

22 Berry, P. and Franks, T. J., "Women in the World of the Corporate Business: Looking at the Glass Ceiling," *Contemporary Issues in Education Research* 3, no. 2 (2010): 1-9.

23 Marshall, J., "Female Leadership and CSR," *Journal of Organizational Change* 20, no. 2 (2007): 165-181.

24 Werhane, P. H., "Women Leaders in a Globalized World," *Journal of Business Ethics* 74, (2007): 425-435.

25 Berry and Franks, "Women in the World of Corporate Business."

26 Bromley, H. R. and Kirscher-Bromley, V. A., "Are You a Transformational Leader?" *Physician Executive* 33, (2007): 54-57.

27 Bolman, L. G., & Deal, T. E., *Reframing Organizations: Artistry, Choice, and Leadership,* 4th ed. (San Francisco, CA: Jossey Bass, 2008).

28 Lineham, M. and Scullion, H., "The Development of Female Global Managers: The Role of Mentoring and Networking," *Journal of Business Ethics* 83, (2009): 29-40.

29 Edwards, C. C., "Entrepreneurship and African American Women: Factors of Success," (PhD diss, 2008).

30 Bates and Loftsrom, "African American's Pursuit."

31 Reaves, B. B., "Entrepreneurial Success: A Phenomenological Study of the Characteristics of Successful Female Entrepreneurs," (PhD diss., University of Phoenix 2008).

32 National Women's Business Council. (2010). Fact sheet. Advisors to the President, Congress, and the SBA. Retrieved from www.nwbc.gov.

33 Welch, B., Martin, D., Martin, W., and Dolowitz, A. R., "A Comparison of Attitudes of Business Training Between African American and White Small Business Owners," *Journal of Business Entrepreneurship* 21, no. 2 (2009): 1-18.

[34] Valdez, Z., "The Effect of Social Capital on White, Korean, Mexican, and Black Business Owners' Earnings in the US," *Journal of Ethnic and Migration Studies* 34, no. 6 (2008): 955-973, doi:10.1080/13691830802211265.

[35] Chiloana, G. and Mayhew, W., "Difficulties Encountered by Black Women Entrepreneurs in Accessing Training from Small Enterprise Development Agency in South Africa," *Gender and Behaviour* 8, no. 1 (2010): 2590-2602.

[36] Serviere, L., "Forced to Entrepreneurship: Modeling the Factors Behind Necessity Entrepreneurship," *Journal of Business and Entrepreneurship* 22, no. 1 (2010): 37-53.

[37] Herbane, B., "Small Business Research: Time for a Crisis-Based View," *International Small Business Journal* 28, (2010): 43-64, doi:10.1177/0266242609350804.

[38] Walker. J. E. K., *The History of Black Business in America: Capitalism, Race, Entrepreneurship: Vol. 1. To 1865,* 2nd ed. (Chapel Hill: University of North Carolina Press, 2009).

[39] Bann, C. L., "An Innovative View of the Entrepreneur Through Exploration of the "Lived Experience" of the Entrepreneur in Startup of the Business," *Journal of Business and Economic Studies* 15, no. 2 (2009): 62-82, 104.

[40] Kidane, A., & Harvey, B. H. Profile of Black Entrepreneurs: Identifying Factors That Discriminate Between Their Levels of success. *Review of Business Research*, 10, no. 1 (2010): 54-64.

[41] Rhodes, C. and Butler, J. S., "Understanding Self-Beliefs of Business Performance: An Examination of Black American Entrepreneurs," *Journal of Developmental Entrepreneurship* 9, no. 1 (2004): 55-71.

[42] Kusmer, K. L. and Trotter, J. W., *African American Urban History Since World War II*, (London, UK: University of Chicago Press, (2009).

[43] Cummings, S., "African American Entrepreneurship in the Suburbs: Protected Markets and Enclave Business Development," *Journal of American Planning Association* 50, (1999): 50-61.

44 Edelman, L. F., Brush, C. G., Manolova, T. S., and Greene, P. G., "Start-Up Motivations and Growth Intentions of Minority Nascent Entrepreneurs," *Journal of Small Business Management* 48, no. 2 (2010): 174-196.

45 U.S. Small Business Administration, "*The Small Business Economy: A Report to the President*," (Washington, DC: U.S. Government Printing Office, 2010).

46 Kusmer and Trotter, "African American Urban History."

47 Gepp, A., Kumar, K. & Bhattacharya, S., "Business Failure Prediction Using Decision Trees," *Journal of Forecasting*, 29, no. 6 (2010): 536-555, doi:10.1002/for.1153.

48 Lussier, R. N. and Halabi, C. E., "A Three-Country Comparison of the Business Success Versus Failure Prediction Model," *Journal of Small Business Management* 48, (2010): 360-377.

49 Horner, M., "Toward an Understanding of Achievement Related Conflicts in Women," *Journal of Social Issues* 28, no. 2 (1972): 157-176.

50 Senchak, M. and Wheeler, L., "Fear of Success in the Social Domain," *Journal of Clinical and Social Psychology* 6, no. 34 (1988): 398-407.

51 Tomkiewicz, J., Bass, K., and Vaicys, C., "Fear of Success and Fear of Appearing Incompetent: A Study of African American Women Business Aspirants," *International Journal of Management* 23, no. 1 (2006): 78-85.

52 Moustakas, C., *Phenomenological Research Methods*, (LOCATION: Sage Publications, 1994).

53 Horner, M. Toward an Understanding of Achievement Related Conflicts in Women. *Journal of Social Issues,* 28, no. 2 (1972): 157-176.

54 "Attitude." In Merriam-webster.com, Accessed April 2019. https://www.merriam- webster.com/dictionary/attitude.

55 Tolle, Eckhart, *The Power of NOW: A Guide to Spiritual Enlightenment.* (Vancouver, B.C. 2004).

56   Gaille, B., "History Timeline of the Entrepreneur and Small Business." Accessed 2019. http://www.history-timeline-the-entrepreneur-and-small-business

57   Welch, B., Martin, D., Martin, W., & Dolowitz, A. R. A Comparison of Attitudes of Business Training Between African American and White Small Business Owners. *Journal of Business Entrepreneurship*, 21, no. 2 (2009): 1-18.

58   Arnold Schwarzenegger, "The New Encyclopedia of Modern Bodybuilding: The Bible of Bodybuilding, Fully Updated and Revised", p. 412, New York: Simon and Schuster, 2012).

59   Jakes, T. *Night Seasons God Still Speaks.* (2006, DVD) Christianity Potter's Touch.

60   Thomas, B., "Achieving success: A phenomenological study of the characteristics of successful African American female entrepreneurs,"(PhD diss., University of Phoenix, 2012).

61   Hooper, T., Metro-Goldwyn-Mayer Film Co., & SLM Entertainment. (1982). *Poltergeist.* S.l.: s.n.

62   U.S. Small Business Administration, (2020), certify.sba.gov

63   Kiva Organization. (2020), About Kiva. https://www.kiva.org/about

64   Kim, W. Chan and Mauborgne, Renée. *Blue Ocean Strategy: How to Create Uncontested Market Space and Make the Competition Irrelevant.* (Boston, Mass.: Harvard Business School Press, 2005).

Made in the USA
Columbia, SC
18 October 2020